Plant & Planet

Goodful

Plant
& Planet

Sustainable & Delicious
Vegetarian Cooking
for Real People

RODALE
BOOKS

New York

Contents

Introduction

When we talk about food—like, really talk about it—there are so many thorny issues. Environmental impact, food justice, fair trade, sustainability, humane practices. It can feel overwhelming, to the point where cracking an egg for breakfast becomes a political act. How can you even begin to unravel all the interconnected systems of food production and distribution? What can you, as one person, really do to make a lasting impact?

This might come as a shock, but the answer is incredibly simple. All it takes are small, intentional steps to make a big impact. There's no need to take on the weight of the world; just pick one, four, ten little adjustments and—here's the important part!—stick to them. A repeated action over time yields amazing results. And as one thing becomes a new habit, then you're ready for a new adjustment, and another, and another, until you're comfortably living more sustainably.

One simple step that we can all start taking today is incorporating more plants into our diet. A strictly vegetarian or vegan diet is a journey and a choice, and we're in no way judging meat eaters. But for everyone looking to cut back, explore new options, expand your palate, boost your health, get out of a rut, or choose any of the millions of reasons to incorporate more plant-based food in your routine, great news! You hit the jackpot with these 75 easy, incredible, and approachable recipes, from delicious drinks (page 191) to ideas that clear out the pantry (page 143); recipes with 5 ingredients or fewer (page 75) to meals ready in less than 10 minutes (page 95); ways to pickle, preserve, and pulverize your produce (page 211) to smart meal preps for a week of delicious options (page 45); bread to break and butter to pass (page 227) to zero-waste recipes that are kind of amazing (page 119); and, of course, a chapter of plant-based junk(ish) food (page 165) because eating should always be fun.

Throughout the book we also share simple, practical, real-life advice for a better planet. You'll find guidance on looking at produce through a seasonal lens (page 13), adding sustainable practices to your grocery shopping (page 17), taking easy steps to reduce packaging (page 25), saving money by cutting back on food waste (page 29), dipping a (green) thumb into gardening (page 35), and making your food last (page 39). And we asked some of our favorite food people—DeVonn Francis, Lorena Ramirez, Lauren Singer, Nadiya Hussain, Kelis Rogers, Ben Flanner, and David Zilber—to weigh in with their experience, helpful advice, and unique perspective on living more sustainably.

From these two pillars—plant and planet—we can all slowly shift our focus to a more natural, impactful, and integrated way of thinking about our habits. By connecting with our food, we connect with our planet. And by connecting with our planet, we connect with our food. The link between plant and planet is a constant, interconnected loop. A small, intentional step of visiting a local farmers' market just once a month opens up the possibility for conversation, education, and— best of all!—discovering produce you've never tried before. Digging all those unused canvas totes out of your closet makes an enormous impact on the environment. Eating a plant-based meal once a day or three times a week or twenty days a month sends you down a new path of awareness. Starting a small pot of herbs, or filling some jars with pickles, or planning your grocery trips for maximum effectiveness are all tiny steps to reducing food waste, increasing environmental impact, and living a more sustainable life. And that's a life we can feel good about.

How to Use This Book

Everything in this book is a guide, not a rule. Cooking should be fun, intuitive, and educational. So dive in and make mistakes!

Each recipe gives you the how-to, but many of the recipes are simply outlines to get your imagination started. Treat them like the blueprints they are and build on them! Everyone makes substitutions for any number of reasons; use what you have on hand or what rings your bell in the moment. Whatever you do, *don't* run to the store just to follow everything to the letter. After all, the spirit of sustainability is getting creative and using what you have.

This is a vegetarian cookbook, meaning we're putting the spotlight on plants but keeping dairy and eggs around, too. Why? Because the simplest, most effective way to reduce your environmental impact is to cut out meat. For any recipe where there's an easy vegan swap, we've noted it. And many of the vegan recipes can easily sub in dairy if vegan cheese isn't your thing. Some recipes are firmly one or the other (sorry!), but most of them can be either.

We've measured out beans by the can as well as by the cup in case you have cooked ones at the ready. Same for other common canned goods like tomatoes. If you're wondering how sustainable any given recipe is, just look right below it. There's a

quick guide to remind you that you're probably already doing better than you realize. And here, there, and everywhere are little notes to help guide you in cooking while easily reducing your environmental impact.

The point is, do what you can, but don't get in your head about it. Keep it light, keep it plant-based, keep it true to you. And most of all, keep it delicious.

Stocking a Sustainable Kitchen

The goal in a sustainable kitchen is to lean heavily toward fresh produce and pantry staples, and away from processed or overly packaged foods. Instead of striving for perfection, aim for improvements. Keep plenty of dried beans on hand (see page 66) for meal prep, but also stock canned beans for nights you just can't even. Fresh fruit is incredible, but frozen fruit is packed at its peak and it's perfect year-round. The same goes for frozen vegetables, which can be the fastest way to add more plant-based nutrition to a meal. There's nothing wrong with a shortcut! (It's still better than takeout.) Here's what to expect to find in heavy rotation in this book.

BAKING

Baking powder

Baking soda

Granulated sugar

Light brown sugar

Coconut sugar

Vanilla extract

Raw honey

Maple syrup

CANNED GOODS

Beans: black beans, chickpeas

Canned tomatoes

Vegetable stock

CONDIMENTS

Dijon mustard

Oils: extra-virgin olive oil, refined coconut, vegetable

Tahini

Tamari

Vinegars: apple cider, red wine, rice, white wine

White miso

DRY GOODS

Beans: black, cannellini, chickpea, kidney, pinto

Coconut flakes

Grains: basmati rice, brown rice, buckwheat, bulgur, farro, jasmine rice, oats, quinoa

Lentils

Pasta, including couscous

Raw nuts: cashews, pecans, walnuts

Seeds: chia, flax, hemp, sesame

FLOURS

All-purpose

Whole wheat

Bread flour

Almond flour

Chickpea flour

FREEZER

Assorted frozen fruits: blackberries, blueberries, cherries, raspberries, strawberries

Assorted frozen veggies: broccoli, peas, vegetable mixes

FRIDGE

Butter of choice

Cheese: feta, mozzarella, Parmesan

Eggs

Greek yogurt

Milk of choice

Yogurt of choice

SEASONINGS

Kosher salt (we used Diamond Crystal throughout this book)

Black pepper

Chili powder

Dried oregano

Ground coriander

Ground cumin

Ground turmeric

Smoked paprika

Shopping Seasonally

Shopping seasonally can be a hard adjustment because we live in a world where everything is available all the time. Do you *need* to make peach cobbler in the middle of winter? No way! But do you sometimes just *need* the comfort of a peach cobbler in the middle of winter? Absolutely. (Are peaches ever worth it in the middle of winter? Pffft, no, but that's a personal choice.)

So here's the deal: Do what you can. Adjust your eating over time to flow with the seasons, but don't expect perfection right away. Find the farmers' markets, roadside stands, or food co-ops in your area. Join a CSA! Use what you find out in the world, not in the weird time-vacuum of a grocery store.

Sure, sometimes, for whatever reason, you just need something that isn't in season right now. And that is just fine because sustainable eating *is not about punishing yourself.* Gwyneth Paltrow won't descend from the clouds and strike you with a lightning bolt. But the next time you're reaching for that pale-pink tomato in early March, keep these three things in mind:

1. **Seasonal produce tastes better.** It just does. When something is allowed to grow in its prime time, it shines.

(A real shine, not the waxy sheen it gets while flying across the globe.)

2. **Buying in season supports sustainable farming practices.** When farmers aren't forcing growth out of season, they use less fertilizer, pesticides, herbicides, water, and energy. You know why? Because nature!

3. **Shopping local is good for everyone.** It puts money in the pockets of farmers. It keeps sustainable agriculture practices alive. It saves you serious cash by cutting out the middleman. It is an all-around smart investment.

So how do you know what's in season? What should you expect to find now, and what will you have to enjoy later? An incredible resource is the Seasonal Food Guide, and it's literally the bomb dot com (no, jk, it's actually seasonalfoodguide.org). You can search by month and region to find exactly what's in season for you this very second. Expect to see seasonal produce used in intuitive ways throughout this book, plus some advice on easy swaps when fresh produce + recipe cravings don't align.

For the purposes of this book, we're going to take a more broad and generalized view of seasonal availability. According to the USDA, a typical—but not exact!—American produce cycle looks something like this:

Spring

Apples	Carrots	Lettuce	Rhubarb
Apricots	Celery	Limes	Spinach
Asparagus	Collard greens	Mushrooms	Strawberries
Avocados	Garlic	Onions	Swiss chard
Bananas	Kale	Peas	Turnips
Broccoli	Kiwifruit	Pineapples	
Cabbage	Lemons	Radishes	

Summer

Apples	Cantaloupe	Green beans	Plums
Apricots	Carrots	Honeydew melon	Raspberries
Avocados	Celery	Lemons	Strawberries
Bananas	Cherries	Lima beans	Summer squash
Beets	Corn	Limes	Tomatillos
Bell peppers	Cucumbers	Mangoes	Tomatoes
Blackberries	Eggplant	Okra	Watermelon
Blueberries	Garlic	Peaches	Zucchini

Fall

Apples	Collard greens	Limes	Radishes
Bananas	Cranberries	Mangoes	Raspberries
Beets	Garlic	Mushrooms	Rutabagas
Bell peppers	Ginger	Onions	Spinach
Broccoli	Grapes	Parsnips	Sweet potatoes
Brussels sprouts	Green beans	Pears	Swiss chard
Cabbage	Kale	Peas	Turnips
Carrots	Kiwifruit	Pineapples	Winter squash
Cauliflower	Lemons	Potatoes	
Celery	Lettuce	Pumpkin	

Winter

Apples	Celery	Limes	Pumpkin
Avocados	Collard greens	Onions	Rutabagas
Bananas	Grapefruit	Oranges	Sweet potatoes
Beets	Kale	Parsnips	Swiss chard
Brussels sprouts	Kiwifruit	Pears	Turnips
Cabbage	Leeks	Pineapples	Winter squash
Carrots	Lemons	Potatoes	

Shopping Sustainably

The hardest question when shopping sustainably is knowing which labels to trust. You know what we're talking about—there's organic, non-GMO, all-natural, cage-free, grass-fed, certified humane, and on and on.

The good news is the answer is very simple. In almost (almost!) all cases, the USDA Organic label is the one that counts. Of all the labeling bodies, the USDA is the toughest on the holy trinity: environmental sustainability, animal welfare, and GMOs. Sometimes packaged foods will have organic *elements* noted in the ingredient list and that's great. Support them! But any food prominently featuring the word *organic* without the USDA seal is making a false claim. (The one exception is small-batch producers or farmers selling directly to consumers. They can claim it without having to certify, so ask for more info on their organic practices.)

The other major label that sustainable and plant-based shoppers often look for is the Non-GMO Project Verified label. This is an uncompromising single-issue label (GMOs are the single issue in question . . . just saying it out loud in case you're lost). But it lacks guidelines on almost everything else. So that beautiful non-GMO heirloom eggplant (yay!) could very well be riddled with pesticides and chemicals (oh no!). In other words:

- Not all non-GMO is USDA Organic, but . . .
- All USDA Organic is non-GMO.

If you have to choose one, go with USDA Organic.

Label terms like "Natural," "Pesticide Free," "Free Range," "Cage Free," "Natural," "Pasture-Raised," "Vegetarian Fed," "Grain-Finished," and "Humanely Raised" are unregulated claims made by the producer. Without a labeled certification, like the excellent Animal Welfare Approved, they are effectively meaningless.

Let's dig deeper into some food categories.

Produce

Again, USDA Organic is the best all-around. This label guarantees:

- The crop was produced without industrial pesticides or ionizing radiation.
- It is non-GMO.
- No antibiotics, synthetic fertilizers, or sewage sludge was used.
- Biodiversity was maintained.

The other label to look for is Certified Naturally Grown (CNG). This collective of farmers peer-reviews and offers organic certification, based on the same exacting guidelines of the USDA, without all the bureaucratic paperwork and insane fees of the National Organic Program. While the USDA

is the watchdog for larger agricultural operations, CNG offers small farmers credit for the work they're doing to sustain local communities. Ask about this label when shopping at markets, co-ops, and farm stands.

Just FYI, two items that are difficult to certify are honey and mushrooms. CNG is working on a mushroom regulation, and they already offer organic certification to small apiaries, which is who you should be buying your delicious local honey from anyway.

Eggs

Again, USDA Organic is the label to look for. It guarantees:

- Non-GMO animal feed
- No hormones at all, and antibiotics only for sick animals
- A cage-free environment
- A chemical-free pasture

The Certified Naturally Grown label follows the same guidelines.

Where both of these labels fall short is in some humanity regulations, especially for "spent" hens, chickens who are no longer laying eggs and are often sold to slaughterhouses or cruelly killed.

Animal Welfare Approved by A Greener World is the best for ensuring your eggs came from a humane environment. They guarantee:

- Non-GMO animal feed
- No hormones at all, and antibiotics only used in illness
- The most comprehensive requirements for a natural and safe life cycle

Dairy

Dairy is difficult because no single label covers the trifecta of animal welfare, environmental impact, and chemical-free in a comprehensive way. The best ones to look for are:

Certified Grassfed by A Greener World

PROS

- All grass-fed
- GMO-free
- Pasture-raised
- No hormones at all, and antibiotics only for sick animals
- The most stringent guidelines for animal welfare

CONS

- No regulation on chemical-free feed
- No regulation on a chemical-free pasture

Pennsylvania Certified Organic Grass-Fed

PROS

- All grass-fed
- Chemical-free feed
- GMO-free
- Pasture-raised
- Chemical-free pasture
- No hormones at all, and antibiotics only for sick animals

CONS

- Relaxed standards for animal welfare

Northeast Organic Farming Association Certified Organic Grass Fed

PROS

- All grass-fed
- Chemical-free feed
- GMO-free
- Pasture-raised
- Chemical-free pasture
- No hormones at all, and antibiotics only for sick animals

CONS

- Very relaxed standards for animal welfare

USDA Organic or CNG

PROS

- Chemical-free feed
- GMO-free
- Pasture-raised
- Chemical-free pasture
- No hormones at all, and antibiotics only for sick animals

CONS

- Grass-fed is not required
- Very relaxed standards for animal welfare

In terms of milk alternatives, moving away from animal products is environmentally beneficial, but every alt-milk has a complicated web of crop production, water footprint, and nutritional value to consider. Of the big three—almond, oat, and soy milk—almond milk fares the worst. It uses a ton of water and has very little nutritional value, but takes minimal land space. In some ways, oat milk is the best, with a low water footprint and a high nutritional value, but the chemical treatments of oat crops are often dangerous, so buying organic or non-GMO is important. In most ways, soy milk is the best option, especially if buying a brand that is organic and uses US- and Canadian-grown soy. Soy is a beneficial crop for the soil, but it takes up a massive amount of land (sometimes in the rain forest, which is why sourcing is important). It uses minimal water but can be sprayed with harmful chemicals, which is why organic is important. But most of all, it's packed with protein and often fortified with other beneficial vitamins and minerals, making it an excellent milk alternative. There is a lot of variation within each brand of each variety of milk, so do some research and find what works best for you!

Where every food label unfortunately falls short is the human cost of food production. Food Justice Certification by the Agricultural Justice Project is a small but mighty label on a mission to fix that. It guarantees living wages, health insurance, fair trade, and high ethical standards for farm workers. In more good news: A farm must already be certified organic to qualify for the Food Justice Certification. So watch for this label to gain visibility and importance in the coming years.

Something that is better than any label is talking face-to-face with the people who made your food. A farmers' market is the best place to get access to the employees responsible for the produce, eggs, and dairy you're about to buy. Not all farms are able to afford organic certification or adhere to strict organic practices, so start a dialogue. Some important questions to ask are:

- Do you use any organic processes?
- What pest control methods do you use?
- Are your animals humanely raised?
- Do you feed your cows anything besides grass and hay?
- Do you feed your chickens a natural diet?

Most important, do not be a Karen at the farmers' market. Be patient with the staff manning the table, who might not have all the answers. Or maybe the farm's practices don't perfectly align with the Sustainable Ideal. Remember that supporting small farmers gives them the capital to work toward more sustainable practices, if that's in their long-term goals. As with everything, small steps make big impacts.

Joining a CSA (Community Supported Agriculture) is another great way to have a dialogue about your food. In a CSA, members buy into a weekly share of fresh, seasonal produce during the growing season. Some CSAs also offer eggs, cheese, and milk in the shares. You'll get direct information from the farm, have lots of new produce to explore, and directly support sustainable agricultural practices. It's a big win all around!

Shopping Package-Free

Package-free shopping in its purest form is the complete elimination of all packaging. Food, beauty products, and even cleaning supplies are bought and stored with little to no unnecessary packaging. For those of us not quite ready for such a huge shift, we can all start—right now! today! this very second!—with one simple change that makes an enormous impact.

Go to your closet and dig out every promotional tote bag you own. Stash some in your car, in your purse, in your backpack, and start using them. Every time you shop, say no thanks to a bag and use your own. It's that easy.

Not to get too tangled up in bags, but this is super interesting. According to the United Nations, somewhere between 1 and 5 trillion plastic bags are used globally each year. Each! Year! In the United States alone, we blow through roughly 380 billion plastic bags and food wraps annually. In 2017 that came out to 4.14 million tons of plastic bags. Three million tons ended up in landfills. In! One! Year! From there, light and playful bags love to hop on the breeze like it's the express train and zip over to every tree, wide-open space, and body of water in sight. Do you get how horrifying this is? Buckle up, it gets worse.

Many natural materials go through biodegradation. But plastics and synthetic materials go through a process called photodegradation, which means they break down into smaller and smaller pieces but never go away. It's hard to measure exactly how much plastic ends up in our oceans, but the evidence is in the animals it's slowly killing. In 2019, a young whale was found dead, starved to death by the almost 90 pounds of plastic blocking his system. More than half of all dead sea turtles are found with plastic in their stomachs. Fish, seabirds, and freshwater wildlife all consume particles of plastic, mistaking it for food.

So ditch plastic for the tote! Once you get into the rhythm with reusable bags, here are five easy ways to increase your impact:

1. **Switch to reusable straws.** Let's be honest, paper straws *suck*. And plastic straws are one of the biggest pollutants. So invest in a set of reusable ones that you can take from home to the coffee shop.

2. **Use a refillable water bottle.** We should all be drinking more water anyway, so keeping one of these nearby helps refresh your body *and* the world around you.

3. **Cook more.** Like the 75 nutritionally dense, sustainably focused, plant-based recipes in this book!

4. **Buy whole foods.** Like the ingredients for the 75 nutritionally dense . . . just kidding. But think of it this way: The more processing and packing something has gone through, the worse it is for your body and the planet.

5. **Use cloth instead of paper.** Buy a set of linen napkins and superabsorbent kitchen towels, and you can permanently cross paper towels off your grocery list.

For a deeper dive into reducing waste, an excellent resource is Litterless (Litterless.com), which offers a list of sustainable online retailers, package-free and bulk stores, and compost sites, all sorted by city and state.

A Sustainable Budget

According to the USDA, we spend an average of 9.7 percent of our disposable income on food. (It's split almost down the middle into 5 percent on groceries and 4.7 percent for delivery and dining out.) That's a sharp contrast to the 1950s, when the average American household was spending nearly 30 percent of their budget on food.

The 1950s, with its uh-oh gender politics and questionable dietary choices, is no one's culinary ideal. But it is interesting to see how the emphasis on where we spend our money has shifted over time. In our modern days of easy access and reliable supply chains, a budget of under 10 percent is reasonable for many people. But a certain thoughtfulness to investing in your food is key to a sustainable budget. Here are five easy ways to make a sustainable budget:

1. **Eat out less.** Not only does it save energy, water, food waste, and garbage, but it also saves you money.

2. **Embrace variety.** Getting stuck in a predictable pattern of eating and shopping will only encourage you to spend more on unnecessary stuff. Keep your kitchen exciting and your meals fresh with new ideas.

3. **Keep a shopping list on your phone.** As you run out of something, add it to the list. Set the habit and stick to it. It'll save you from buying duplicates or making a return trip for the one thing you forgot (and then picking up three things you don't need).

4. **Meal prep!** Even if it's not making actual meals, take a day to make a huge pot of rice, cook a few varieties of dried beans, make your own nut milk, or wash and chop vegetables. One hour in calm mode is the equivalent of six hours in starving mode.

5. **Don't aim for perfection.** Eat out when you need to, or even want to, but check in periodically and make sure your food budget is always going mostly toward sustainable practices.

The best way to spend less is to shop more often. The average American throws away about 238 pounds of food each year, so buy small quantities of perishables more frequently to save money in the long run. Start dividing your shopping into monthly, weekly, and daily categories.

Monthly

Pantry staples like grains, pasta, beans, cereals, nuts, and spices should be purchased monthly. Same with any condiments. If you need something before the month is up, dig in your pantry to see what you could use in its place. Don't go buy black beans when you have pintos at home!

Weekly

Things like milk, eggs, cheese, and other items in the (non)dairy aisle should be on weekly rotation. If you're not using up these things within the week, buy smaller amounts or go biweekly.

Daily

Everything fresh and highly perishable like fruits and vegetables should be purchased on the daily. Not literally every day, but every few days as needed. If you're a CSA member or a weekly farmers' market is part of your schedule, then load up for the week and make sure everything is stored properly (see page 41 for advice on that) to prevent early spoilage. Any additional produce you need should be purchased as close to the day of use as possible.

But in all of your shopping, limit yourself to things you need. Don't overbuy and don't get ambitious. A market full of gorgeous spring produce is so inspirational, but if you know you have plans a few nights this week, resist the urge to load up. Shop for what you will actually eat tomorrow, not what you want to eat right now.

In an ideal world we'd all be domestic deities who have limitless time to make everything from scratch. But as our lives are increasingly pressed for time, buying premade, canned, or frozen foods in this day and age is not a sin against sustainability. A few frozen (but organic!) meals to save time is no sweat. We love canned beans! (Sometimes even more than making them from scratch, but you didn't hear that from us.) And frozen fruits and vegetables are always the way to go for maximum flavor if you're buying in the off-season. There's no shame in taking some shortcuts for sanity's sake. Our one request is that your decisions continue leaning toward sustainable practices and not away from them.

Forbes recently did a study comparing the costs of delivery and meal kits against the cost of shopping for ingredients at Whole Foods to make the same meals from scratch. They found, on average, delivery meals were five times more expensive and meal kits were three times more expensive than simply cooking for yourself. (Not to mention the environmental costs saved.) So chew on that the next time you're looking at your budget.

Grow Your Own

Growing a garden is like learning to cook, with all the patience, care, and satisfaction. But like learning to cook, it takes time and practice (and some failures) to get it right.

For those of you lucky enough to have outdoor space, a full garden might be in your future. For those of you in apartments, something fun like a homegrown lettuce or pepper plant might be in your future. But for everyone starting out, do yourself a favor and go slow!

For every thumb that is flesh-colored but dying to be green, we suggest starting with an herb garden. Think of it as your training wheels, a pilot program, the herbs that walked so your string beans could run, etc. Here's how to get started:

1. **The first thing to consider is location, location, location.** Some herbs, like basil, thyme, and rosemary, enjoy lots of light. Chives, parsley, and mint like it but don't need it. So find a place that will suit a variety of needs. A windowsill is a great place, as is any surface that gets sunlight. A stoop or balcony that has shady areas is wonderful. And if you're short on space, look up. Suspending a tension rod across your window is a great way to hang some growing baskets.

2. **Procure some pots.** These can really be anything at all, from actual pots to reused glass, metal, or plastic containers (sustainability!). Just make sure the pot is at least six inches in diameter to allow for sturdy root growth. If there's no drainage hole at the bottom, layer a few inches of small rocks or pebbles in the lower quarter of the pot so your roots don't rot.

3. **Next is potting soil.** Actual potting soil. Don't dig up dirt from outside (runoff chemicals, dog pee, you just don't know!). Avoid gardening soil (too heavy and it'll crush your delicate babies!). So invest in a natural, organic potting soil. Also invest in some sand, for better drainage, and compost. Toss two parts potting soil, one part sand, and one part compost in a large container, then loosely fill your pots.

4. **Pick two or three herbs.** We all want an abundant, verdant, green goddess fantasy to welcome the morning, but come back to earth for a second. When you have a small group of healthy and thriving herbs, then you can add more to your rotation. But for now, take the minimal approach.

The best for growing indoors are:

Mint	
Parsley	Fine with shade and want damp soil with more frequent waterings
Chives	
Basil	
Rosemary	Love sunlight and want dry soil between waterings
Thyme	

5. **Plant one herb per pot to give them maximum room and let them set their own rules.** You know, just because rosemary and thyme both love the sun, they don't necessarily make great roommates. (We've all lived with a rosemary.) Growing from seed can be a long and frustrating process, so don't be ashamed to start with small herb plants.

6. **As your herbs grow, get in there and trim them.** They're there to eat, after all! Use a pair of scissors to trim at the stem, cutting only from the newer growth at the upper levels of the plant. Don't cut more than a third of the plant at a time, and allow it to regrow before your next trimming.

Once you get the hang of a few herbs, add some more. Then add some easy vegetables like scallions, spinach, or microgreens. And finally start exploring more complex vegetables like tomatoes, peppers, and strawberries. Before you know it, you'll be a green machine!

Almost every natural thing that passes through your kitchen can be returned to the earth (if not repurposed) in a smart, sustainable way. Compost is a nutrient-dense soil that makes miracles grow without the chemicals. Most farmers' markets have a compost bin, and if they don't, ask where you can donate scraps. Litterless (Litterless.com) also offers a list of compost sites by city and state, if you're shy.

Start introducing the idea of reducing garbage in easy phases.

Phase 1

Store vegetable scraps (ends, peels, stems, greens) in an airtight container in your freezer to make stock. (For a list of good stock scraps, see page 127.) After they're boiled to death, those scraps can go right back in the freezer for Phase 2.

Phase 2

Save all nondairy food scraps (vegetable scraps, fruit scraps, rice, pasta, bread, cereal, coffee grounds, coffee filters, tea bags, eggshells, nut shells) in your freezer to donate to a compost collection.

Phase 3

Start saving other biodegradable materials (flowers, dead plants, potting soil from your failed herbs) in your freezer, plus paper and cardboard packaging, to donate to a compost collection.

Phase 4

Start building your own compost pile. This is truly next-level and you will need a compost bin and worms. When you're ready for this level, you'll seek the guidance you need.

Now get out there and get growing!

Make It Stretch

Nearly 40 percent of food goes to waste in the United States. That's way too close to half to feel comfortable about it. In producing all that unused food, we also lose about 20 percent of land, fertilizer, and water, and generate the equivalent of 37 million cars' worth of greenhouse gases. So . . . yikes!

Shopping seasonally, sustainably, package-free, within budget, and growing your own all make an enormous impact. The final step is reining in food waste by effectively using what you have. To prevent food spoilage, take the time to store wisely.

Let's start with the refrigerator and freezer, keeper of many things. Go out now and buy a cheap fridge thermometer and make sure you're staying below 40°F at all times (37°F is the ideal). The freezer should be kept at 0°F, aka freezing. Your next purchase is glass or eco-friendly storage containers. (Reusing plastic take-out containers is a very eco-conscious move, too.) And your final purchase is a roll of masking tape and a permanent marker to keep in a kitchen drawer. Every single thing in your fridge and freezer will now get a tape label with its name and a date.

When storing food in the refrigerator, leave plenty of room (you should be buying only what you need anyway, remember?) for cold air to circulate easily. And adopt a first in, first out mentality. New food goes to the back and food that needs to be eaten now comes up front. Refrigerators go from most cold at the bottom to least cold at the top, so think about your unit in zones:

- **The door:** This is the worst place to keep things cold, so get your eggs and milk away from this zone! Condiments, pickles, and sauces all belong here.

- **Upper shelves:** Anything already cooked can go here, like snacks, leftovers you plan to eat soon, and meal prep. Dairy products and eggs can go here if you plan to use them quickly.

- **Lower shelves:** Dairy products and eggs should really go here if there's room. Fruits and vegetables that belong in the fridge (we'll get to that list in a second) go here, too.

- **Crisper drawers:** If you have them, this is an even better place for the most delicate fruits and vegetables, like greens, carrots, cucumbers, and berries.

- **The freezer:** Anything for long-term storage, like leftovers, premade meals, frozen fruits and vegetables, or uncooked foods that are nearing expiration and need a lifeline.

- **On top:** Nothing, since it might give off heat! It'll only spoil food, even nonperishables like cereal.

When it comes to fresh produce, the easiest rule of thumb is to store them as they were at the grocery store. But if you forget (or you're buying produce only from farmers' markets), here's a reminder what that looks like!

Refrigerator

Things like asparagus, beets, bell peppers, blueberries, broccoli, Brussels sprouts, cabbage, carrots, cauliflower, cherries, grapes, green beans, herbs, leeks, lettuce and salad greens, mushrooms, peas, raspberries, strawberries, and zucchini.

Room Temp*

Things like apples, avocados, bananas, cucumbers, eggplant, garlic, grapefruit, lemons, limes, mangoes, melons, nectarines, onions, oranges, peaches, pears, pineapple, plums, potatoes, shallots, squash, and tomatoes.

Herbs

Soft herbs, like cilantro, dill, mint, and parsley, should be stored like a flower bouquet in a glass of water. Place them in the refrigerator on a lower shelf and change the water every other day. Basil can be stored in a glass of water on the counter. (The harsh cold of a refrigerator will turn basil leaves black.)

Hardy herbs, like chives, oregano, rosemary, sage, and thyme, should be loosely wrapped in a damp paper towel. Stack the bundles in an airtight storage container and store in the crisper drawer.

---

* All the room-temp fruit can be moved to the fridge if it's ripening too fast, but do not store in the crisper drawer. They give off a gas called ethylene that will spoil the other fruits and vegetables.

Fresh herbs should last at least 1 week when stored properly.

Pantry items to care for are nuts, whole grains, and grain flours, which have a high oil content and can spoil quickly. They're best stored in airtight containers in the fridge (top shelf is fine) to extend their life indefinitely.

And speaking of spoilage, oils needs love and care, too. Many oils can go rancid fairly fast, so buy small containers for things you use less frequently and moderate sizes of containers for things you use often. And as nice as it is to have oil within reach when cooking, do not store it in a cupboard above your oven or directly next to your stove. The radiant heat will only speed up the spoilage.

All other pantry items such as grains, beans, rice, pasta, and spices can be kept somewhere cool and dry, like a cupboard or—wouldn't you know it!—a pantry. But be mindful of what you have in order to prevent buying duplicates or letting them sit too long. Even nonperishables do eventually perish.

For everything fresh that's nearing extinction, learn to preserve them—pickles, jams, dehydrated fruit, dried herbs, and hot sauces. And a good old toss in the freezer is another great way to rescue things from the brink or simply stretch summer fruit to last all winter. For more info, refer to The Preservation Society (page 211), a whole chapter devoted to everything you need to know.

Work Smarter, Not Harder

Three breakfasts, three lunches, plus an essential guide to the building blocks—grains, beans, and roasted veggies—to meal-prep your week with plant-based goodness.

Falafel with Ginger Slaw

Who doesn't love falafel? This recipe might seem like a lot of steps, but 90 percent of it is just running things through the food processor. At the end, you'll have a bright and zingy slaw, two delicious sauces, and crispy-on-the-outside-soft-on-the-inside falafel for lunch or dinner. Effort today, grateful tomorrow. And the next day. And the day after that. You get it.

Slaw

1-inch piece fresh ginger, peeled

2-inch piece carrot, scrubbed

3-inch wedge red cabbage

2 scallions, thinly sliced

2 tablespoons finely chopped fresh parsley

1 tablespoon white wine vinegar

1 tablespoon olive oil

1 teaspoon sugar of choice or raw honey

½ teaspoon kosher salt

½ teaspoon freshly ground black pepper

Falafel

2 (15.5-ounce) cans chickpeas, drained and rinsed, or 1 pound dried chickpeas, soaked overnight and drained

1 large shallot, quartered

4 garlic cloves, smashed

10 sprigs fresh parsley, stems and leaves, cut into 1-inch pieces

10 sprigs fresh cilantro, stems and leaves, cut into 1-inch pieces

2 teaspoons ground coriander

2 teaspoons ground cumin

2 teaspoons kosher salt

1 teaspoon chili powder

¼ cup chickpea flour

2 teaspoons baking powder

Sauces

Juice of 1 lemon

¼ cup plain yogurt of choice

2 sprigs fresh cilantro, stems and leaves

2 tablespoons olive oil

1 teaspoon kosher salt

¼ cup tahini

Assembly

Vegetable oil, for deep-frying (about 2 quarts)

8 whole wheat pitas, quarters

1. **Make the slaw:** Grate the ginger into a medium bowl. Set up the shredding disc in a food processor. Process the carrot into grated pieces and add to the bowl with the ginger. Process the cabbage into grated pieces and add to the bowl. Add the scallions, parsley, vinegar, oil, honey, salt, and pepper and toss to combine. Cover tightly and place in the refrigerator to marinate.

WORK SMARTER, NOT HARDER • 47

2. **Make the falafel:** If using canned chickpeas, preheat the oven to 450°F.

3. Spread the canned chickpeas out on a sheet pan. Place them in the oven and turn the heat off. Let the chickpeas dehydrate in the oven for about 30 minutes, until mostly white and dried. (If using dried chickpeas that have been soaked, skip this step.)

4. Meanwhile, in the same food processor, add the shallot, garlic, parsley, cilantro, coriander, cumin, salt, and chili powder. Pulse about 10 times, scraping down the sides as needed, to form a pesto-like paste. Add the chickpeas and pulse about 10 more times, scraping down the sides as needed, to form a crumbly mixture.

5. Transfer the mixture to a medium bowl and add the chickpea flour and baking powder. Use clean hands to incorporate everything into one cohesive, slightly sticky dough. Cover the bowl and place in the refrigerator for 30 minutes.

6. **Make the sauces:** In the same food processor (it's okay if little raw falafel gets in the sauce), add half of the lemon juice, the yogurt, cilantro, olive oil, and ½ teaspoon of the salt. Process for about 30 seconds to form a cohesive sauce with small pieces of cilantro. Transfer to a small bowl, cover, and place in the refrigerator.

7. In the same food processor (it's okay if a little yogurt gets in the sauce), add the tahini, the remaining lemon juice, the remaining ½ teaspoon salt, and ¼ cup cold water. Process for about 30 seconds to form a smooth sauce. Transfer to a small bowl, cover, and place in the refrigerator.

8. **To assemble:** Pour 2 inches oil into a large Dutch oven or saucepan and heat over medium-high heat to 325°F.

9. While the oil heats, line a plate with paper towels. Use clean hands to form the mixture into 16 falafel balls and set on the lined plate. If the mixture is too crumbly to hold together, add more water, 1 teaspoon at a time.

10. Working in batches, use a slotted spoon to lower the falafel into the oil. Fry until the falafel are deeply browned, about 5 minutes. Use the slotted spoon to return them to the paper towels to drain. Divide the falafel among four storage containers. Divide the slaw, sauces, and pita segments into the containers. Store in the refrigerator for up to 1 week.

Notes • To use up that ginger, carrot, and cabbage, see Kraut (page 216) or Spicy Braised Cabbage (page 156).

PLANT
This recipe is vegan.

PLANET
Grab your produce from the farmers' market or shop package-free in your grocery's produce section. Buy your spices and chickpeas from bulk bins for bonus points.

NUTRITION, Falafel, without pita, per serving

| Calories: 874 | Carbs: 66 g | Fiber: 18 g |
| Fat: 61 g | Protein: 21 g | Sugar: 12 g |

NUTRITION, Ginger Slaw, per serving

| Calories: 58 | Carbs: 7 g | Fiber: 2 g |
| Fat: 4 g | Protein: 1 g | Sugar: 3 g |

NUTRITION, Lemon Yogurt Sauce, per tablespoon

| Calories: 70 | Carbs: 1 g | Fiber: 0 g |
| Fat: 7 g | Protein: 1 g | Sugar: 1 g |

NUTRITION, Tahini Sauce, per tablespoon

| Calories: 45 | Carbs: 2 g | Fiber: 0 g |
| Fat: 4 g | Protein: 1 g | Sugar: 0 g |

Samosa Frittatas

Samosas, a savory Indian pastry, are warm pockets of joy. The stars of a vegetarian samosa—potatoes, peas, and a medley of warm spices—stretch their legs to invigorate a very savory but very breakfastable frittata. A sheet pan frittata is welcoming to a wide array of produce and spices, so once you're mastered the skill, let sustainability take charge and adapt to what you have on hand. Make it one day and enjoy it all week; the flavors only get better over time!

1 large russet potato, cut into ½-inch pieces

2 tablespoons olive oil or refined coconut oil

2 teaspoons kosher salt

¼ cup vegetable stock, store-bought or homemade (page 126)

12 large eggs

1 cup milk of choice

8 sprigs fresh cilantro, coarsely chopped (stems and leaves)

½ teaspoon chili powder

½ teaspoon ground coriander

½ teaspoon ground cumin

½ teaspoon ground ginger

½ teaspoon ground turmeric

½ teaspoon freshly ground black pepper

¼ teaspoon ground cardamom

1 cup fresh or frozen peas

1 medium shallot, finely chopped

Chutney (opposite), for serving

1. Set a rack in the center of the oven and preheat to 400°F.

2. In a medium bowl, toss together the potato, 1 tablespoon of the oil, and 1 teaspoon of the salt. Spread the potatoes in a 9 × 13-inch baking pan and add the vegetable stock. Bake until the potatoes are tender, about 20 minutes.

3. Meanwhile, in a medium bowl, whisk together the eggs, milk, cilantro, chili powder, coriander, cumin, ginger, turmeric, black pepper, cardamom, and remaining 1 teaspoon salt.

4. When the potatoes are cooked, use a fork to lightly smash. Add the peas, shallot, and the remaining 1 tablespoon oil to the baking pan. Toss the oil with the vegetables, then pour the egg mixture over the vegetables. Stir to evenly distribute everything across the pan.

5. Bake until the eggs are set and slightly puffy, 15 to 20 minutes. Cool for about 10 minutes and then slice into 4 even pieces. Divide the pieces into storage containers and store in the refrigerator for up to 1 week. Serve with a healthy drizzle of the chutney.

Chutney · Makes ½ cup

6 fresh mint leaves

2 sprigs fresh cilantro

1-inch piece ginger, peeled

1 garlic clove

1 jalapeño, halved and seeded

2 tablespoons vegetable oil

Add the mint, cilantro, ginger, garlic, jalapeño, vegetable oil, and 2 tablespoons water to a blender. Blend on high for about 1 minute, scraping down the sides as needed, until the mixture is smooth. Transfer the chutney to a storage container and refrigerate for up to 1 week.

PLANT
This recipe is vegetarian.

PLANET
Potatoes are commonly available year-round, and frozen peas can carry you through the off-season.

NUTRITION, Frittata, per serving

Calories: 427	Carbs: 30 g	Fiber: 5 g
Fat: 23 g	Protein: 26 g	Sugar: 5 g

NUTRITION, Chutney, per serving

Calories: 92	Carbs: 8 g	Fiber: 0 g
Fat: 7 g	Protein: 0 g	Sugar: 5 g

Buckwheat & Berry Parfaits

Serves 4

Buckwheat, despite its name, is not a wheat but a seed. (Weird flex, but okay.) One of the most sustainable crops, it's naturally disease-tolerant, resistant to pests, and a happy home to bees. On top of that, it's packed with fiber, protein, antioxidants, vitamins, and minerals, and a perfect base for a not-too-sweet breakfast loaded with other very smart foods like berries and tahini for good carbohydrates, vitamins, and tons of protein to start your day. Made all at once and stored in the fridge through the week, this is a grab-and-go breakfast that will make you go go go!

2 cups water

1 cup buckwheat

½ teaspoon kosher salt

3 cups berries or cut fruit, fresh or frozen

8 tablespoons tahini

8 tablespoons maple syrup

8 tablespoons milk of choice

Hemp hearts, chia seeds, flaxseeds, or unsweetened coconut flakes, for serving

1. In a medium-large saucepan, bring the water to a boil over high heat. Stir in the buckwheat and salt and return to a boil. Reduce the heat to medium-low and simmer uncovered until the buckwheat is tender, about 10 minutes. Drain.

2. Line up four pint jars with lids. Into each jar, spoon 3 tablespoons cooked buckwheat, ¼ cup fruit, 1 tablespoon tahini, and 1 tablespoon maple syrup. Repeat with another layer of buckwheat, fruit, tahini, and maple syrup. Finish with one more layer of fruit on top. Screw the lids on tightly and store in the refrigerator for up to 1 week.

3. To serve, drizzle 2 tablespoons milk over each parfait and sprinkle with a topping of choice.

PLANT
This recipe can be made fully vegan.

PLANET
Swap in fresh fruit throughout the year or freeze in-season fruit now to enjoy later.

NUTRITION, per serving

| Calories: 449 | Carbs: 62 g | Fiber: 5 g |
| Fat: 21 g | Protein: 11 g | Sugar: 37 g |

Zucchini Lasagna Boats

There's bad news and there's good news here. The bad news is there's no pasta (booo!). But the good news is there's plenty of cheese (yaaay!). Think of it as a zoodle—the naturally package-free pasta—taken to the max. Scooped-out zucchini gets stuffed with a trio of veggies, plus tomatoes and cheese, for a packable lunch that will float your boat all week.

4 large zucchini

4 tablespoons ricotta cheese

1 tablespoon grated lemon zest

Kosher salt

2 tablespoons olive oil

1 garlic clove, minced

5 ounces baby bella (cremini) mushrooms, quartered

1 (14.5-ounce) can diced tomatoes or 1¾ cups diced fresh tomatoes

2 cups baby spinach

4 ounces mozzarella cheese, sliced

4 fresh basil leaves

1. Set a rack in the center of the oven and preheat to 400°F.

2. Cut a ¼-inch-thick slice, lengthwise from stem to end, from each zucchini, exposing the inner flesh. Use a paring knife to cut and a soup spoon to scoop out the flesh, reserving the flesh and leaving a ¼-inch-thick wall. The zucchini should look like four little canoes. Arrange them in a large skillet, supporting one another.

3. In a small bowl, stir together the ricotta, lemon zest, and ½ teaspoon kosher salt. Spread 1 tablespoon of the ricotta mixture along the inside of each zucchini. Set aside.

4. Finely chop the reserved zucchini flesh. In a medium skillet, heat the oil over medium heat until shimmering. Add the zucchini, garlic, and mushrooms and season with a generous pinch of salt. Cook, stirring often, until the zucchini has released liquid and cooked down, about 5 minutes. Add the tomatoes and continue cooking and stirring until the liquid has cooked off, about 5 minutes more. Add the spinach and cook until wilted, about 2 minutes more. Taste for seasoning.

–recipe continues–

PLANT
This recipe is vegetarian, but swap in vegan cheeses to make it fully plant-based.

PLANET
Produce can be purchased at the farmers' market, or shop package-free in your grocery's produce section. Zucchini is at its peak freshness in the summer months.

NUTRITION, per serving

Calories: 235	Carbs: 14 g	Fiber: 5 g
Fat: 16 g	Protein: 13 g	Sugar: 8 g

5. Spoon the mixture into the zucchini boats, packing them and filling them to the top. (Cool any leftover filling and transfer to a storage container. Refrigerate for up to 1 week or freeze for up to 6 months for a quick pasta sauce.)

6. Add ¼ cup of water to the skillet, transfer to the oven, and bake until the zucchini is tender, about 15 minutes. Remove the zucchini from the oven and cover in the mozzarella slices. Set the oven to broil and place the skillet under the broiler until the mozzarella is browned and bubbling, 2 to 3 minutes.

7. Cool the zucchini completely and top each one with a basil leaf. Transfer to separate storage containers and refrigerate for up to 1 week or freeze for up to 3 months.

Mushroom al Pastor Bowls

Serves 4

Mushrooms are such a star player in vegetarian cooking because they can hold up to almost any cooking method and still retain a meaty bite. Quickly sautéed and cooked in a spicy (and easy) al pastor sauce, they're the star of a ready-in-a-flash bowl that's as customizable as ordering a burrito bowl from an app, but a much cheaper way to get through the week.

Mushrooms & salsa

2 (10-ounce) packages baby bella (cremini) mushrooms

2 tablespoons olive oil

1 teaspoon smoked paprika

1 teaspoon chili powder

2 teaspoons kosher salt

½ teaspoon freshly ground black pepper

2 (8-ounce) cans crushed pineapple or 2 cups cut fresh pineapple

1 (7-ounce) can chipotle peppers in adobo sauce

1 garlic clove, peeled

1 tablespoon dried oregano

2 teaspoons ground cumin

½ cup lager beer or water

PLANT
This recipe is vegan.

PLANET
Mushrooms are most commonly found at the farmers' market in the spring and fall months. This recipe also leans heavily on common pantry items, so dig through your cupboards before shopping.

For serving

2 cups hemp hearts

4 cups cooked brown rice
(see Grains for the Week, page 64)

½ white onion, thinly sliced

2 radishes, thinly sliced

¼ cup finely chopped fresh cilantro

1. **Make the mushrooms:** Rip the mushrooms, stems included, by hand to create uneven pieces, about ½ inch to 1 inch. In a Dutch oven, heat the oil over medium heat until shimmering. Add the mushrooms and cook, stirring occasionally, until the mushrooms release and evaporate their liquid and are starting to brown on the bottom of the Dutch oven, about 15 minutes. Add the smoked paprika, chili powder, 1 teaspoon of the salt, and the black pepper. Cook for 1 minute more until the spices are fragrant.

2. **Meanwhile, make the salsa:** In a food processor, combine the pineapple, chipotles plus adobo sauce, garlic, oregano, cumin, and remaining 1 teaspoon salt. Process for about 1 minute until the chipotles are broken down and a chunky salsa forms.

3. When the mushrooms are starting to brown, add ½ cup of the salsa and the beer to the Dutch oven. Use a wooden spoon to scrape all the browned bits from the bottom of the Dutch oven. Cook for about 2 minutes until the sauce is thickly coating the mushrooms.

–recipe continues–

4. To serve: Stir the hemp hearts into the cooked brown rice. Divide the rice mixture, cooked mushrooms, onion, radishes, and cilantro among four storage containers. Spoon some of the salsa over the top for an extra spicy meal, or transfer the salsa to a storage container and refrigerate for up to 1 week (or freeze for up to 6 months). Refrigerate the prepared meals for up to 1 week.

NUTRITION,
Mushrooms al Pastor with salsa, no rice

Calories: 550	Carbs: 104 g	Fiber: 20 g
Fat: 12 g	Protein: 12 g	Sugar: 38 g

NUTRITION, Mushrooms al Pastor only,
per serving (not including salsa)

Calories: 329	Carbs: 48 g	Fiber: 4 g
Fat: 11 g	Protein: 11 g	Sugar: 0 g

NUTRITION, Salsa, per 2 tablespoons

Calories: 121	Carbs: 32 g	Fiber: 3 g
Fat: 0 g	Protein: 1 g	Sugar: 23 g

Squash Breakfast Bowls

Serves 4

Acorn squash is harvested in the late summer and fall, but thick-skinned squashes keep for months after, which is why they're grouped in a category called winter squash. (Butternut, spaghetti, delicata, and pumpkin are all common examples.) Use fresh fruit that is currently in season, or pull from your freezer to enjoy perfect berries in the middle of winter. Packed with tons of fiber, vitamins, minerals, antioxidants, and protein, this is a smarter bowl than fruity flaky chunks of cereal.

Squash

2 medium acorn squash
(1 to 1½ pounds each)

2 tablespoons olive oil or refined coconut oil

2 teaspoons kosher salt

Per each breakfast

1 tablespoon maple syrup

1 teaspoon ground cinnamon

¼ cup cut fruit or berries, fresh or frozen

2 tablespoons toasted nuts, coarsely chopped

2 tablespoons milk of choice

1. Set a rack in the center of the oven and preheat to 400°F.

2. **Make the squash:** Halve each squash lengthwise and scoop out the seeds. Season the cut sides with the oil and salt. Set the squash flesh-side down in a 9 × 13-inch baking pan. Pour 1 cup water into the pan and bake the squash until a knife easily slides into the flesh, about 1 hour. Remove from the pan and cool completely. Transfer the 4 cooked squash bowls to storage containers and refrigerate for up to 1 week.

3. **Make each breakfast:** To each squash bowl, add the maple syrup and cinnamon. Use a spoon to scrape and mash the flesh, incorporating the maple syrup and cinnamon, but keeping the bowl shape of the rind intact. To serve cold, sprinkle the fruit and nuts on top of the squash, then add the milk. To serve warm, scoop the mashed flesh out of the squash (leaving the rind intact) and combine in a small saucepan with the milk. Cook for 2 to 3 minutes, stirring occasionally, to warm through. Return the squash to its bowl and finish with the fruit and nuts.

Note • Leftovers can be refrigerated for up to 1 week.

PLANT
This recipe can be made fully vegan.

PLANET
Squash has a broad seasonal life. Swap in fresh fruit throughout the year or freeze now to enjoy later.

NUTRITION, per serving

| Calories: 444 | Carbs: 74 g | Fiber: 17 g |
| Fat: 17 g | Protein: 9g | Sugar: 17 g |

Grains for the Week

Makes 3 cups

There is nothing better—literally nothing—than having precooked grains waiting in the refrigerator. Grains are among the least water- and energy-intensive crops, so treat yourself and the planet right by setting aside a designated grain day every week. Pro tip: Always start by thoroughly rinsing your grains in a mesh sieve until the water runs clear. This will remove any residue or excess starch. Then grab a large saucepan and get ready to cook!

- **Cooked grains will keep in the refrigerator for up to 5 days.** Frozen grains will keep for up to 6 months.

- **To freeze, spread the cooked grains on a sheet pan lined with parchment paper.** Allow the grains to cool completely. Transfer the pan to the freezer, careful that it stays level. Freeze for about 2 hours, until completely frozen, then fold the parchment paper to pour the grains into a freezer-safe container. Let them sit overnight in the refrigerator to thaw. Do not refreeze thawed grains.

PLANT
This recipe is vegan.

PLANET
Start a habit of bringing a reusable container and buying your grains in bulk. A mason jar or even an upcycled plastic container is the perfect vessel to go straight from store to storage.

Grain	Water	Salt	Notes
1 cup basmati rice	1½ cups water	½ teaspoon kosher salt	Add the rice, water, and salt to a saucepan. Bring to a boil over high heat, then cover and reduce the heat to medium-low. Simmer for 15 minutes. Remove from the heat and let it steam, still covered, for 10 minutes. Fluff with a fork.
1 cup brown rice	2 cups water	½ teaspoon kosher salt	Add the rice, water, and salt to a saucepan. Bring to a boil over high heat, then cover and reduce the heat to medium-low. Simmer for 45 minutes. Remove from the heat and let it steam, still covered, for 10 minutes. Fluff with a fork.
1 cup buckwheat	2 cups water	½ teaspoon kosher salt	Bring the water to a boil over high heat. Stir in the buckwheat and salt. Reduce the heat to medium-low and simmer uncovered for about 10 minutes, until tender. Drain thoroughly.
1 cup bulgur	2 cups water	½ teaspoon kosher salt	Bring the water to a boil over high heat. Stir in the bulgur and salt. Cover and remove from the heat. Steam the bulgur for 20 to 30 minutes, until tender and fluffy. Drain any excess water and fluff with a fork.
¾ cup couscous	¾ cup water	½ teaspoon kosher salt	Bring the water to a boil over high heat. Stir in the couscous and salt. Cover and remove from the heat. Steam the couscous for about 10 minutes, until tender and the liquid is absorbed. Fluff with a fork.
1 cup farro	4 cups water	½ teaspoon kosher salt	Add the farro, water, and salt to a saucepan. Bring to a boil over high heat, then reduce the heat to medium-low. Simmer uncovered for 30 to 40 minutes, adding more water as needed, until tender. Drain thoroughly.
1 cup jasmine rice	1½ cups water	½ teaspoon kosher salt	Add the rice, water, and salt to a saucepan. Bring to a boil over high heat, then cover and reduce the heat to medium-low. Simmer for 15 minutes. Remove from the heat and let it steam, still covered, for 10 minutes. Fluff with a fork.
1 cup quinoa	1¾ cups water	½ teaspoon kosher salt	Add the quinoa, water, and salt to a saucepan. Bring to a boil over high heat, then cover and reduce the heat to medium-low. Simmer for 15 minutes. Remove from the heat and let it steam, still covered, for 10 minutes. Fluff with a fork.

Beans for Days

There is nothing better—literally nothing—than having precooked beans waiting in the refrigerator. (If you're having déjà vu about the grains, just remember that two things can be true at once.) Pro tip: Always start by thoroughly rinsing your beans or lentils in a mesh sieve, picking out any stones or broken beans. Beans take about 2 hours, including a 1-hour soak, and lentils are ready in under an hour with no soak necessary. Red and yellow lentils are much better cooked as part of a dish—usually as a thickener for soups or curries—so they're not included here. As a protein source, beans and lentils are not only cheaper and better for you, but they're also water-efficient and great for the soil, setting them far ahead of animal and processed soy proteins!

- **Cooked beans will keep in the refrigerator for up to 5 days.** Frozen beans will keep for up to 6 months.

- **To freeze, spread the cooked beans on a sheet pan lined with parchment paper.** Allow the beans to cool completely. Transfer the pan to the freezer, careful that it stays level. Freeze for about 2 hours, until completely frozen, then fold the parchment paper to pour the beans into a freezer-safe container. Let them sit overnight in the refrigerator to thaw. Do not refreeze thawed beans.

PLANT
This recipe is vegan.

PLANET
Start a habit of bringing a reusable container and buying your beans in bulk. A mason jar or even an upcycled plastic container is the perfect vessel to go straight from store to storage.

Variety	Salt	Aromatics	Notes
1 cup black beans	1 tablespoon plus ½ teaspoon kosher salt	1 medium piece kombu, ½ white onion, 4 garlic cloves, 1 medium carrot (halved), 1 celery stalk (halved)	Add the beans, 1 tablespoon of salt, and 2 quarts cold water to a Dutch oven. Bring to a boil over high heat, then remove from the heat and soak uncovered for 1 hour. While the beans soak, set a rack in the center of the oven and preheat to 275°F. Drain and rinse the soaked beans, then return them to the pot with 2 quarts of cold water. Add the aromatics and remaining ½ teaspoon salt. Bring to a boil over high heat, then cover and transfer to the oven. Bake for 40 minutes to 1 hour, until 5 beans selected at random are tender.
1 cup cannellini beans	1 tablespoon plus ½ teaspoon kosher salt	1 medium piece kombu, ½ white onion, 4 garlic cloves, 2 sprigs rosemary, 1 medium carrot (halved), 1 celery stalk (halved)	
1 cup chickpeas	1 tablespoon plus ½ teaspoon kosher salt	1 medium piece kombu, ½ white onion, 2 sprigs parsley, 4 garlic cloves, 1 medium carrot (halved), 1 celery stalk (halved)	
1 cup kidney beans	1 tablespoon plus ½ teaspoon kosher salt	1 medium piece kombu, ½ white onion, 4 garlic cloves, 1 medium carrot (halved), 1 celery stalk (halved)	
1 cup pinto beans	1 tablespoon plus ½ teaspoon kosher salt	1 medium piece kombu, ½ white onion, 2 sprigs thyme, 4 garlic cloves, 1 medium carrot (halved), 1 celery stalk (halved)	
1 cup black lentils	½ teaspoon kosher salt	½ leek (quartered), 2 garlic cloves, 2 sprigs rosemary	Set a rack in the center of the oven and preheat to 325°F. Add the lentils, salt, aromatics, and 4 cups water to a medium pot and cover. Transfer the pot to the oven and bake for 40 minutes to 1 hour, until 5 lentils selected at random are tender.
1 cup brown lentils	½ teaspoon kosher salt	½ leek (quartered), 2 garlic cloves, 2 sprigs rosemary	
1 cup French green lentils	½ teaspoon kosher salt	½ leek (quartered), 2 garlic cloves, 2 sprigs rosemary	
1 cup green lentils	½ teaspoon kosher salt	½ leek (quartered), 2 garlic cloves, 2 sprigs rosemary	

Roasting Veggies

There is nothing better—literally nothing—just kidding! When it comes to veggies, sometimes it *is* better to cook them on the spot. But for busy weeks or an abundance of produce, roasting in batches makes for an easy mix-and-match to boost any meal. Here is an (almost) comprehensive guide to roasting veggies.

Everything can be roasted on a sheet pan with enough olive oil to lightly coat, a generous pinch of salt, and a few cracks of black pepper. Be sure not to overload the pan; leaving some room between the vegetables allows them to roast perfectly. Always rotate the pan front to back and toss the vegetables halfway through baking for even browning.

- Leftovers can be refrigerated for up to 1 week.

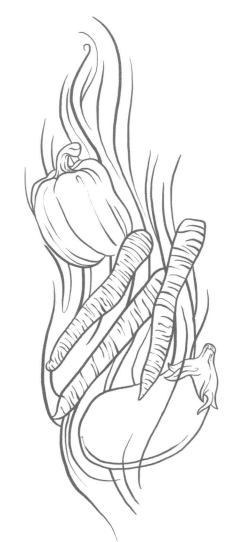

PLANT
This recipe is vegan.

PLANET
Pack those canvas totes and hit the farmers' market. It's the perfect place to find inspiration, discover new produce, and expand your repertoire.

Vegetable	Oven Temperature	Prep	Minutes
Asparagus	400°F	Whole, ends trimmed	10 to 15
Beets	400°F	Whole, wrapped in foil (peel and cut when cooled)	50 to 60
Bell peppers	450°F	Whole (after roasting, cover tightly until skin peels away easily)	20 to 30
Broccoli	400°F	Florets	20 to 30
Brussels sprouts	450°F	Trimmed, halved	20 to 30
Carrots	450°F 450°F	Whole 1-inch pieces	20 to 30 15 to 20
Cauliflower	425°F 450°F	Florets Whole	20 to 30 50 to 60
Eggplant	400°F 400°F 350°F	Peeled and cubed 1-inch steaks, skin on Whole, about 1 pound	30 to 40 30 to 40 50 to 60
Fennel	425°F	Fronds removed, cut into wedges	20 to 30
Garlic	375°F	¼ inch off the top of the head, wrapped in foil	40 to 50
Leeks	400°F	Halved, washed, cut into 1-inch pieces	20 to 30
MUSHROOMS			
Chanterelle	400°F	Whole, cleaned	10 to 15
Cremini	400°F	Halved, cleaned	10 to 15
Morel	400°F	Whole, cleaned	10 to 15
Oyster	425°F	Whole, cleaned	40 to 50
Portobello	450°F	Stems trimmed, roast stem-side up	10 to 15
Shiitake	400°F	Stems removed	20 to 30
Onions	400°F	Peeled and cut into wedges	30 to 40

–chart continues–

Vegetable	Oven Temperature	Prep	Minutes
Parsnips	425°F	Peeled and cubed	30 to 40
Potatoes	400°F	Peeled and cubed	25 to 30
	400°F	Wedges, skin on	25 to 30
	425°F	Whole, pierced with a fork	40 to 50
Rutabagas	425°F	Peeled and cubed	30 to 40
Shallots	400°F	Peeled and halved	30 to 40
	425°F	Whole, skin on	50 to 60
Squash			
Acorn	450°F	Halved, seeds scooped out, cut into wedges	30 to 40
Butternut	450°F	Peeled, halved, seeds scooped out, cut into cubes	20 to 30
Delicata	450°F	Halved, seeds scooped out, cut into rings	20 to 30
Kabocha	450°F	Halved, seeds scooped out, cut into wedges	30 to 40
Spaghetti	450°F	Halved, seeds scooped out, roast cut-side down	30 to 40
Sugar pumpkin	400°F	Halved, seeds scooped out, roast cut-side down	30 to 40
Sweet potatoes	400°F	Peeled and cubed	25 to 30
	400°F	Wedges, skin on	25 to 30
	425°F	Whole, pierced with a fork	40 to 50
Turnips	250°F	Peeled and cubed	20 to 30

DeVonn Francis

Chef, Artist &
Founder of Yardy World

It's the summer of 2002. There's
the feeling of a fresh strawberry's
balloon-like tautness, just before
it bursts at the seams, between
my tongue and the pressure of
my teeth. I am standing in a field
in Pungo, Virginia. Strawberry
picking is an hour spent in
neat rows that appear as long

as the sky feels wide. Having to do the harvesting myself every year around that same time with friends and family hearkens back to the peak of summer.

It was here I first learned that seasonal eating—and connecting to the labor of the land—is the highest investment in yourself. The heat index is well above 80 degrees, a harbinger for beach picnics, roasted corn on the grill, and backyard Slip 'N Slides. Postharvest, my aunt—a seasoned entertainer—would roll the strawberries around in sugar and cinnamon, gently massaging the fruit until the white sandy sweet became a pool of pink fruit juice. Dessert is served on little ceramic dishes with painted roosters all around the rim. The platter is well worn, with text that faintly reads "Welcome Home."

My memories of home initially attracted me to the art of entertaining. When I host parties now, I'm drawing from a lifetime of spirited family gatherings and lively summer meals at all-day August block parties. The connecting thread that runs through all of my favorite occasions is the feeling that food is a transportive memory. One bite can take you through cultural experiences, miles and miles away, and at the very same time connect you to the feeling of being right at home. My past twenty-seven summers have a smell, taste, sound, and tactility I let run wild in my mind every time I tie my apron and lift my knife.

Food is inherently social. You find your way through the flavor of any season by nosing through markets and picking up conversations in earshot about the latest song, style, and dance. For me, the greatest reward comes from taking time to connect to the faces and personalities behind my food, asking questions, learning something more every time. Each season returns with familiar signals: the crisp of apples during the fall, a heft of winter savoy, and the snap of tender spring peas. I still get inspired by the shift in weather and how it impacts what is available around us—at our dinner table, grocery stores, and the farms where our food grows, the needs of our communal and individual health shift together.

Much like seasons, memories reappear on their own cycle. And just as the promise of macerated strawberries piled high fades away to crunchy leaves and the swish of a trench coat repelling wind, the image of getting up for a second slice of sweet potato pie comes in to readily take its place not too long after. We eat for pleasure and to remind ourselves of where we are in time, relying on our senses as inspiration to recall how we got to where we are in the first place.

A Lot with a Little

Easy meals with just 5 ingredients
(plus oil, salt, and pepper)!

Miso Ramen Noodles

Serves 2

A mixture of miso and butter, things you probably have sitting in your refrigerator, punch up a packet of ramen noodles with all the desired savory notes. (Bonus: No more hunting down the one vegetarian pack! Double bonus: Buy the noodles in larger quantities without the package at an Asian grocery store.) Kimchi, a versatile ingredient that can keep for several months in the fridge, adds a nice textural crunch, and a sprinkle of scallions brings some bite. Five ingredients that are greater than the sum of their parts!

4 tablespoons (½ stick) unsalted butter of choice

¼ cup white miso

2 (3-ounce) packages instant ramen (seasoning packets reserved for another use like salad dressings or sprinkling over roasted veggies)

1 cup kimchi, coarsely chopped

2 scallions, thinly sliced

1. In a medium saucepan, combine the butter, miso, and 2 cups water and bring to a boil over high heat. As the water heats, stir the butter and miso to melt.

2. When the water is boiling, add the ramen. Cook for 3 minutes, stirring often to break up the noodles, until tender. Remove the saucepan from the heat and stir in ¾ cup of the kimchi. Divide the ramen and sauce between two bowls. Top with the remaining kimchi and the scallions. Serve immediately.

Note • Leftovers can be refrigerated for up to 1 week.

PLANT
This recipe is vegan.

PLANET
If scallions aren't in season, get creative with herbs like cilantro or basil. Everything else might be sitting in your pantry already.

NUTRITION, per serving

| Calories: 288 | Carbs: 12 g | Fiber: 4 g |
| Fat: 26 g | Protein: 6 g | Sugar: 3 g |

Sweet Potato Toasts

Serves 3 to 6

There's no real replacement for the delicious crunch of toast. But a sliced sweet potato, browned and warm from the toaster, is nothing to scoff at. It adds a firm, delicious base for pretty much any topping (not to mention being more sustainable than the resources that go into making bread). To us, a mixture of bitter frisée, a sweet-savory dressing, and a creamy egg yolk seemed like the perfect place to start, but you do you.

1½ pounds sweet potatoes

1 tablespoon fresh lemon juice

2 tablespoons tahini

½ teaspoon kosher salt

4 cups frisée

6 large eggs

Freshly ground black pepper

1. Slice a thin piece from one long side of the sweet potato to create a flat surface. (Save that piece for Vegetable Scrap Stock, page 126.) Lay the flat surface against the cutting board and cut the sweet potatoes lengthwise into 6 even toasts, about ¼-inch-thick pieces.

Working with 2 at a time, place the toasts in a toaster set to the maximum heat. When it pops, flip the toasts over and toast again. Flip them one more time and toast until the sweet potato has started to brown. Transfer them to a wire rack to cool while toasting the remaining sweet potato. (Alternatively, the toasts can be baked in a 350°F oven for about 15 minutes, directly on the oven rack, with a flip halfway through.)

2. Meanwhile, in a medium bowl, whisk together the lemon juice, tahini, salt, and 2 tablespoons water. Add the frisée and toss to coat. Set aside.

3. Bring a large skillet filled with 1 inch of water to a boil over high heat. Working with one at a time, crack an egg into a small bowl. Lower the rim of the bowl into the skillet of boiling water and gently tip the egg in. Repeat with the remaining 5 eggs. Cook the eggs until the whites are set but the yolks are still soft, 2 to 4 minutes. Use a slotted spoon to remove the eggs to a paper towel to drain.

4. Set 1 or 2 toasts on each plate, divide the frisée among the toasts, and lay a poached egg on top of each toast. Finish with a few grinds of black pepper.

Note • Eat it right away. Alternatively, store the greens, sweet potato toasts, and dressing separately in the refrigerator for up to 1 week, poaching the eggs and assembling as needed.

PLANT
This recipe is vegetarian, but omit the eggs to make it fully plant-based.

PLANET
Sweet potatoes and hearty salad greens like frisée can be found at the farmers' market in the fall or winter months. Feel free to swap any other greens that are available.

Brussels Sprout Salad

Serves 4

We all know roasted Brussels sprouts are crispy, dreamy perfection. But have you taken a deep dive into raw Brussels sprouts? Because, listen, they are also perfect. Thinly sliced, they add just the right kind of slaw-like crunchy base, ready to take on big flavors. Flavors just like these: warm butternut squash, toasted hazelnuts, and zingy pickled shallots. Yum!

1 medium shallot, thinly sliced

3 tablespoons red wine vinegar

½ pound butternut squash, peeled and cubed (about 2 cups)

1 tablespoon olive oil

Kosher salt and freshly ground black pepper

½ cup hazelnuts

1 pint Brussels sprouts (about 8 ounces)

1. Set a rack in the center of the oven and preheat to 450°F.

2. In a small bowl, toss together the shallot and vinegar and set aside to marinate.

3. Toss the squash and oil on a sheet pan. Season with a generous pinch of salt and plenty of pepper. Bake until the squash is tender and starting to brown, 20 to 25 minutes, stirring halfway through. In the last 5 minutes of baking, add the hazelnuts to toast.

4. While the squash bakes, thinly slice the Brussels sprouts and add to a large bowl.

5. When the squash and hazelnuts are finished, add them to the large bowl along with the shallot and vinegar. Toss and taste for seasoning, adding salt and pepper as needed.

Note • Leftovers can be refrigerated for up to 1 week.

PLANT
This recipe is vegan.

PLANET
Brussels sprouts and butternut squash are in season together. Feel free to swap in other nuts, like pecans, walnuts, cashews, or peanuts—whatever you have on hand.

NUTRITION, per serving

| Calories: 184 | Carbs: 15 g | Fiber: 5 g |
| Fat: 13 g | Protein: 5 g | Sugar: 4 g |

Charred Whole Broccoli Salad

This dish is the *definition* of a lot with a little. The entire broccoli, from stem to floret, pops in the oven to get tender and charred. Chiles bring the heat, capers bring some brine, raisins add sweetness, and a soft-boiled egg is all the creamy richness you could want. Heaven in a bowl.

1 large head broccoli (about ½ pound)

2 tablespoons olive oil

Kosher salt

2 large eggs

2 Calabrian chiles, coarsely chopped, or 1 teaspoon red pepper flakes

2 tablespoons capers, drained

¼ cup golden raisins or black raisins

Freshly ground black pepper

1. Set a rack in the center of the oven and preheat to 450°F.

2. Use a vegetable peeler to remove the tough outer layer of the broccoli stem. Cut the stem into 1-inch pieces and separate the florets. Add the broccoli florets and stems, oil, and a generous pinch of salt to a sheet pan and toss to combine. Bake until the broccoli is tender and charred in places, 15 to 20 minutes.

3. While the broccoli cooks, bring a medium saucepan of water to a boil over high heat. Gently lower the eggs into the water and boil for 7 minutes. Remove the eggs and rinse under cold water to cool. Gently tap the eggshells and peel, rinsing under cold water again to remove any shell pieces.

4. Transfer the broccoli and any oil on the sheet pan to a medium bowl. Add the chiles, capers, raisins, and a generous pinch of salt. Stir to combine.

5. Divide the broccoli mixture between two bowls. Gently slice the eggs in half and lay them on top of the salad. Season the eggs with a small pinch of salt and finish with a few grinds of black pepper.

Note • Leftovers can be refrigerated for up to 1 week.

PLANT
This recipe is vegetarian, but omit the eggs to make it fully plant-based.

PLANET
Broccoli can be found at the farmers' market in the spring or fall months. Everything else might be sitting in your pantry already.

NUTRITION, per serving

| Calories: 279 | Carbs: 23 g | Fiber: 3 g |
| Fat: 19 g | Protein: 9 g | Sugar: 14 g |

Grilled Fruit & Corn Salad

Serves 2 to 4

The perfect refreshing side for grilling season (or I-don't-want-to-turn-on-the-oven season if you're cooking in the great indoors). Corn and stone fruit get a quick char before being assembled with an easy basil vinaigrette. It's a light, smoky, punchy salad that just screams, "I LOVE SUMMER!"

1 tablespoon refined coconut oil or vegetable oil

2 ears of corn, husked and halved

4 pieces of stone fruit, such as peaches, apricots, nectarines, or plums, halved and pitted

¼ cup olive oil

10 fresh basil leaves

2 tablespoons white wine vinegar

Kosher salt

1. Preheat a grill to medium-high for at least 20 minutes. (Alternatively, heat a grill pan or 12-inch cast-iron skillet over medium-high heat until smoking.)

2. Brush the grill (or skillet) with the coconut oil. Lay the corn pieces and the fruit halves, cut-side down, over the heat. Grill, rotating the corn, until nicely charred in places, 5 to 7 minutes.

3. Meanwhile, in a food processor, combine the olive oil, basil, vinegar, and ¼ teaspoon salt and pulse 5 times until the basil is finely chopped.

4. Arrange the grilled fruit on a serving platter. Use a fork to hold one corn piece vertically on a cutting board. Run a knife along the ear to release the kernels. Continue to rotate the corn to remove all the kernels. Repeat with the remaining pieces of corn.

5. Sprinkle the kernels over and around the grilled fruit. Season with a small pinch of salt. Spoon the basil mixture over the salad and serve immediately.

Note • Leftovers can be refrigerated for up to 1 week.

PLANT
This recipe is vegan.

PLANET
Buy your corn and stone fruit in the summer months when they're at peak freshness. Your palate and planet will thank you.

NUTRITION, per serving, based on 4 servings

| Calories: 258 | Carbs: 25 g | Fiber: 4 g |
| Fat: 18 g | Protein: 3 g | Sugar: 16 g |

Savory Oatmeal

Although oatmeal is often seen as a breakfast food, just like a bowl of cereal it's great any time of day. But unlike boxed cereals, oats are an important part of sustainable crop rotation systems and can be easily purchased in bulk. This savory update justifies its place on a lunch or dinner table, with a quick-pickled shallot, charred cherry tomatoes, and umami-rich tamari. Oatmeal, you've come a long way from apples and cinnamon!

1 medium shallot, thinly sliced

¼ cup red wine vinegar

1 pint cherry tomatoes

2 tablespoons olive oil

1¼ teaspoons kosher salt

1 cup old-fashioned rolled oats

2 tablespoons tamari

1. Set a rack in the center of the oven and preheat to 450°F.

2. In a small bowl, toss together the shallot and vinegar and set aside to marinate.

3. Toss the tomatoes and oil in an 8 × 8-inch baking pan. Bake until the tomatoes burst and are starting to char, about 15 minutes. Remove from the oven and season with 1 teaspoon of the salt.

4. While the tomatoes cook, in a medium saucepan, bring 2 cups water to a boil over high heat. Stir in the oats and remaining ¼ teaspoon salt. Reduce the heat to medium-low and simmer until the oats are tender, about 15 minutes.

5. Divide the oats between two bowls. Drizzle each bowl with 1 tablespoon tamari. Spoon the tomatoes on top. Drain the shallots (save the vinegar for salad dressing!) and sprinkle them on top.

Note • Leftovers can be refrigerated for up to 1 week.

PLANT
This recipe is vegan.

PLANET
Cherry tomatoes are at their best in the summer months. For the rest of the year, substitute 1½ cups cubed butternut squash and add ¼ cup water to the pan when baking. Everything else might be sitting in your pantry already.

NUTRITION, per serving

Calories: 419	Carbs: 15 g	Fiber: 1 g
Fat: 14 g	Protein: 3 g	Sugar: 12 g

Rice Salad with Peas & Radishes

Rice salads are the unsung heroes of the salad family. Hearty and filling, rice is a perfect showcase for seasonal produce and a beautiful vessel for absorbing dressing. This salad leans super fresh with raw sugar snap peas, radish slices, and mint, tossed with rice vinegar. But don't feel limited by the seasonality of this recipe. Go ahead and toss in any produce that's fresh and beautiful during whatever month you're in!

1 tablespoon olive oil

1 cup cooked brown rice
(see Grains for the Week, page 64)

2 tablespoons rice vinegar

Kosher salt

20 sugar snap peas

10 fresh mint leaves, thinly sliced/julienned

4 medium radishes

Freshly ground black pepper

1. In a medium saucepan, heat the oil over medium-high heat until shimmering. Add the rice, 1 tablespoon of the vinegar, and ½ teaspoon salt. Remove from the heat and stir to combine. Set aside to marinate.

2. While the rice marinates, slice the tips of the peas and pull off the tough string along the pod. Cut the pods on the bias into ¼-inch-wide slices. Stack and roll the mint leaves and julienne. Thinly slice the radishes.

3. When the rice is cool, add the prepared vegetables, remaining 1 tablespoon vinegar, a generous pinch of salt, and plenty of pepper. Toss to combine and serve immediately.

Note • Leftovers can be refrigerated for up to 1 week.

PLANT
This recipe is vegan.

PLANET
Radishes and peas are in season in the spring and fall, but swap in other produce like raw zucchini and cucumber in the summer months or roasted root vegetables in the winter months.

NUTRITION, per serving

| Calories: 106 | Carbs: 15 g | Fiber: 3 g |
| Fat: 4 g | Protein: 3 g | Sugar: 1 g |

Greek Fries

Serves 2

Think of these like cheese fries minus the processed orange sauce and the regret. Crispy potato wedges get covered in a tangy yogurt sauce, seasoned with oregano, and finished with feta crumbles. All the pleasure, none of the (stomach) pain!

1 large russet potato (about 1 pound)

1 tablespoon olive oil

1 teaspoon kosher salt

2 tablespoons Greek yogurt

Juice of ½ lemon, plus ½ lemon for serving

2 teaspoons dried oregano

4 ounces feta cheese, crumbled

1. Set a rack in the center of the oven and preheat to 475°F.

2. Cut the potato in half in one direction and then in half in the opposite direction, creating four equal quarters. Cut each quarter into four wedges. Transfer the fries to a medium bowl and fill with hot tap water. Soak for 15 minutes to release some starch, then drain the fries, rinse, and pat dry.

3. In an 8 × 8-inch pan, toss the fries with the olive oil and salt. Tightly cover the pan with foil and bake for 5 minutes. Remove the foil and continue to bake until the fries are tender and nicely browned, 15 to 20 minutes longer.

4. While the fries bake, in a small bowl, whisk together the yogurt, lemon juice, and 1 teaspoon of the oregano.

5. Take the fries out of the oven and sprinkle half of the feta and the remaining 1 teaspoon oregano over them. Spoon the yogurt mixture on top, then finish with the remaining feta. Set the oven to broil and place the pan under the broiler until the feta has slightly browned in spots, 1 to 2 minutes.

6. Serve immediately with the lemon half to squeeze over the top.

Note • Leftovers can be refrigerated for up to 1 week.

PLANT
This recipe is vegetarian, but swap in vegan yogurt and cheese to make it fully plant-based.

PLANET
This recipe leans heavily on common pantry items, so dig through your cupboards before shopping.

NUTRITION, per serving

| Calories: 447 | Carbs: 54 g | Fiber: 6 g |
| Fat: 19 g | Protein: 16 g | Sugar: 6 g |

Lorena Ramirez

Digital Creator, Lifestyle Expert & Founder of Healthy Hyna

I was sitting next to an enormous pig that weighed about 300 pounds. I remember gazing at the grassland as I listened to the pig subtly breathing. I looked into its eyes and I couldn't believe I was unconsciously eating this being of a creature. I didn't feel

superior nor did I feel inferior to this pig. I sensed we were both on the same journey with the desire to love and be loved.

From that day forward, I cut meat out of my diet—completely! At that time a plant-based diet was a radical concept, especially within my community and family. I came home to my mom and told her I was vegetarian. *"¡Estás loca! ¡Vas a comer como los pobres!"* Which translates to: You're crazy! You're going to eat like the poor!

Ever since I was a child, my mom would often retell the stories from when she was a child, one of seven siblings growing up in a small village in Mexico. She would say there was always a shortage of food not only in her household but also within her community. These stories were ingrained in my head. Every time I had scraps of food left over on my plate, she would make a comment that people in Mexico were starving. It made me feel guilty so I would lick the plate clean. I remember gathering every piece of leftover rice with my fork and slurping it so I wouldn't miss a piece. Now, as an adult, I've come to realize how her story about food insecurity made an impact on the way I choose to eat and shop. The amount of resources it takes to grow food can affect the availability of basic foodstuffs for those in other countries, while food production in developed nations is controlled by corporations. There's so much power in shopping with intention; when you shop sustainably, you make a positive contribution to societies across the globe.

Food has set the foundation for me to have a creative career. My curiosity with food was sparked when I started to vegan-ize traditional Mexican dishes, relying on accessible ingredients without the need to shop at a specialty health food store. Seven years later, I'm not only vegan because of my admiration and respect for animals, but also to break from what mainstream society finds to be the social norm. I have the power to pass on new, healthy, and enlightened food cycles to my own daughters and influence my community in a positive, conscious direction. I became vegan to pay my respects to Mother Earth and the environment. But in the process I realized eating a plant-based, vegan diet can also make a positive impact on global issues that stem from unconscious eating, everything from food injustice to environmental impact. Take inventory of the ingredients you currently have on hand and take inventory of your community before you shop for more. Small, intentional steps can start you on the path to positive change.

10 Under 10

Here are 10 meals ready in less than 10 minutes!

Tomato & Pita Salad

Somewhere between a panzanella salad and a Greek salad (okay, kind of right in the middle) sits this salad. Pita slices get quickly toasted and then tossed in a beautiful medley of peak summer produce. A little lemon and a little garlic to keep it all exciting, plus za'atar—a Middle Eastern spice blend of the greatest hits of the Mediterranean—holds down the savory notes. It's a simple dish with a ton of flavor.

3 (7-inch) pocketless pitas

4 tablespoons za'atar

2 tablespoons olive oil

2 garlic cloves, minced

Juice of 1 lemon

4 medium heirloom tomatoes

1 medium red onion

1 large English cucumber

Kosher salt and freshly ground black pepper

1. Set racks in the center and lower third of the oven and preheat to 500°F.

2. Cut the pitas into roughly 1-inch pieces. (Uneven pieces are great!) Spread the pitas over two sheet pans. Bake until the pitas are crisp and toasted, 6 to 8 minutes, rotating the pans front to back and switching racks halfway through.

3. Meanwhile, in a small bowl, whisk together the za'atar and olive oil and set aside. In a large bowl, mix the garlic and lemon juice and set aside to let the garlic mellow.

4. Cut the tomatoes, onion, and cucumber into 1-inch pieces. Add the tomatoes, onion, and cucumber to the bowl with the garlic and toss. Add about half of the za'atar oil, a generous pinch of salt, and several grinds of black pepper. Toss again.

5. As soon as the pitas are toasted, drizzle the remaining za'atar oil over them. Add them to the salad and toss again. Serve immediately.

Note • Eat it right away. Alternatively, refrigerate the toasted pita and salad separately for up to 1 week and assemble as needed.

PLANT
This recipe is vegan.

PLANET
This salad is all about the produce, so you want peak tomatoes and cucumbers at the height of summer. It's worth the wait.

NUTRITION, per serving, based on 6 servings

Calories: 200	Carbs: 41 g	Fiber: 4 g
Fat: 2 g	Protein: 7 g	Sugar: 8 g

Four Seasons Gazpachos

Serves 4

Haters will say these aren't gazpachos. And you know what? They're totally right. But you know what's more fun than being right? Being creative! ("Being seasonal!" is also an acceptable answer.) Four different soups highlighting the stars of the season will have your blender whirring all year. Serve hot or chilled for the perfect meal in a flash.

Spring

1 avocado, halved and pitted

½ pound asparagus, ends trimmed, cut into 2-inch pieces

1 cup spinach

½ cup fresh or frozen peas

1 garlic clove, peeled

Juice of 1 lemon

1 teaspoon kosher salt, plus more to taste

2 tablespoons olive oil, plus more for serving

1. Scoop the avocado flesh into a blender. Add the asparagus, spinach, peas, garlic, lemon juice, salt, olive oil, and 2 cups cold water. Blend on high until a smooth soup forms, about 2 minutes, scraping down the sides as needed. Taste for seasoning.

2. Divide among four bowls and serve with a drizzle of olive oil.

Summer

2 red bell peppers, cut into chunks

1 English cucumber, quartered

½ pound heirloom tomatoes, quartered

½ pound seedless watermelon, cubed

Juice of 1 lemon

1 tablespoon olive oil, plus more for serving

1 teaspoon kosher salt, plus more to taste

1. In a blender, combine the bell peppers, cucumber, tomatoes, watermelon, lemon juice, olive oil, and salt. Blend on high until a smooth soup forms, about 2 minutes, scraping down the sides as needed. Taste for seasoning.

2. Divide among four bowls and serve with a drizzle of olive oil.

Fall

1 small cauliflower, cut into florets

2 celery stalks, cut into 2-inch pieces, leaves reserved for serving

1 large shallot, peeled and halved

1 garlic clove, peeled

Juice of 1 lemon

1 teaspoon kosher salt, plus more to taste

2 tablespoons olive oil, plus more for serving

1. In a medium saucepan, bring 2 cups water to a boil over high heat. Add the cauliflower florets

and boil until tender, about 5 minutes. Remove from the heat and let the cauliflower and cooking water cool for 10 minutes.

2. In a blender, combine the cauliflower, cooking water, celery, shallot, garlic, lemon juice, salt, and olive oil and blend on high until a smooth soup forms, about 2 minutes, scraping down the sides as needed. Taste for seasoning.

3. Divide among four bowls and serve with a drizzle of olive oil and a few celery leaves.

Winter

1 pound beets, scrubbed and quartered

2 medium carrots, scrubbed and cut into 2-inch pieces

1 large leek, dark green tops trimmed off, cut into 2-inch pieces

1 large shallot, peeled and halved

1 garlic clove, peeled

Juice of 1 lemon

1 teaspoon kosher salt, plus more to taste

2 tablespoons olive oil, plus more for serving

1. In a medium saucepan, bring 2 cups water to a boil over high heat. Add the beets and carrots and boil until the carrots are tender and the beets are partially cooked, about 10 minutes.

Remove from the heat and cool in the cooking water for 10 minutes.

2. In a blender, combine the beets, carrots, cooking water, leek, shallot, garlic, lemon juice, salt, and olive oil and blend on high until a smooth soup forms, about 2 minutes, scraping down the sides as needed. Taste for seasoning.

3. Divide among four bowls and serve with a drizzle of olive oil.

Note • Leftovers can be refrigerated for up to 1 week.

PLANT
This recipe is vegan.

PLANET
Get creative and swap in fresh, seasonal produce at peak freshness. Your palate and planet will thank you.

NUTRITION • SPRING GAZPACHO, per serving

Calories: 183	Carbs: 13 g	Fiber: 7 g
Fat: 14 g	Protein: 5 g	Sugar: 3 g

NUTRITION • SUMMER GAZPACHO, per serving

Calories: 83	Carbs: 13 g	Fiber: 2 g
Fat: 4 g	Protein: 2 g	Sugar: 9 g

NUTRITION • FALL GAZPACHO, per serving

Calories: 108	Carbs: 10 g	Fiber: 4 g
Fat: 7 g	Protein: 3 g	Sugar: 5 g

NUTRITION • WINTER GAZPACHO, per serving

Calories: 139	Carbs: 18 g	Fiber: 4 g
Fat: 7 g	Protein: 3 g	Sugar: 12 g

Nori Burritos

If you've never had a seaweed burrito, get ready. Nori, the seaweed used for sushi rolls, is not only packed with vitamins and minerals, but it also doesn't weigh you down like a tortilla. (Not to mention that seaweed is one of the most sustainable crops and tortillas, though delicious, come with a bunch of environmental hurdles.) Fresh veggies, a light dressing, and rice—relax, no one is coming for the rice—make this a deluxe burrito that feels delightful. Investing in a good box grater is a worthy step toward cutting back on the plastic waste of buying preshredded vegetables.

1 avocado

½ medium carrot

1 large asparagus, ends trimmed

1 tablespoon tamari

2 teaspoons white miso

1½ cups cooked rice
(see Grains for the Week, page 64)

2 sheets nori

1. Halve, pit, and peel the avocado. Cut into thin slices. Use the large holes of a box grater to grate the carrot, then grate the asparagus. Set all aside.

2. In a small bowl, whisk together the tamari and miso. Set aside.

3. Microwave the rice for about 30 seconds to warm. Spread ¾ cup of the warm rice on a sheet of nori, leaving a ½-inch border around the edges. Drizzle half of the tamari mixture over the rice. Arrange half of the avocado, asparagus, and carrot on one side of the rice. Tuck in the sides of the nori and begin to roll the nori over the ingredients. With each rotation, pause to tuck in the sides and slide the burrito closer to you. Slice the finished burrito in half. Repeat with the remaining nori, rice, tamari mixture, and vegetables. Serve immediately.

Note • Eat it right away. The wrap won't refrigerate or reheat well.

PLANT
This recipe is vegan.

PLANET
Avocados, carrots, and asparagus all hit their peak in the spring months. Use bell peppers and spinach in the fall or roast some squash in the winter to enjoy these year-round.

NUTRITION, per serving

| Calories: 338 | Carbs: 45 g | Fiber: 8 g |
| Fat: 15 g | Protein: 7 g | Sugar: 2 g |

Quick Bibimbap

Serves 1

Bibimbap, a Korean rice dish instantly recognizable by its rainbow of toppings, is traditionally served in a stone bowl to get a crispy crust on the rice. This at-home swap uses a hot skillet for an almost-as-good effect. This recipe is ideal for things you might already have lying around—leftover rice, pickled vegetables, an egg—and any prepared proteins or quickly sautéed veggies are welcome to join the party. *Bap* refers to cooked rice and *bibim* means "mixed"; once you have your toppings arranged, add a dollop of gochujang and give it all a good mix before diving in. The egg adds a creamy richness to the rice, the gochujang brings a sweet spice, and the crunchy pickles give a bright acidity for a perfect bite every time. It's a brilliant way to clean out your fridge.

1 tablespoon vegetable oil

1½ cups cooked rice
(see Grains for the Week, page 64)

1 large egg

1½ cups various roasted vegetables
(see page 68) or pickles (see page 213),
thinly sliced

Gochujang, for serving

1. In a 6-inch nonstick skillet, heat the oil over medium-high heat until shimmering. Add the rice in an even layer, leaving a hole in the center. Crack the egg into the hole. Cover the skillet and fry until the egg white is set and the rice is crispy on the bottom, 6 to 7 minutes.

2. Remove the skillet from the heat. Arrange the pickled vegetables over the rice. Serve with gochujang.

Note • Leftovers can be refrigerated for up to 1 week.

PLANT
This recipe is vegetarian, but omit the egg to make it fully plant-based.

PLANET
Use those pickles you made when produce was at its peak or make this as an excuse to rescue any dying produce.

NUTRITION, per serving

| Calories: 559 | Carbs: 79 g | Fiber: 5 g |
| Fat: 19 g | Protein: 15 g | Sugar: 3 g |

Vegan Caesar

Croutons are great, sure. But fried chickpeas bring the crunch, pack the protein, and save a trip to the store, a total win-win-win. (And hey, if you have some bread that's going stale, cube it and fry it in place of the chickpeas!) Tossed with a creamy you'd-never-know-it's-vegan dressing plus faux parm crumbles that are 100× more addictive than the green shaker, you have a salad that feels like the main event.

Croutons

1 tablespoon olive oil

1 (15.5-ounce) can chickpeas, drained, rinsed, and dried, or 1½ cups cooked chickpeas (see Beans for Days, page 66), drained and dried

¼ teaspoon kosher salt

Freshly ground black pepper

Dressing

¼ cup Use It Up Hummus (page 150)

Juice of ½ lemon

1 garlic clove, peeled

2 tablespoons olive oil

2 teaspoons Dijon mustard

1 teaspoon tamari

1 teaspoon capers

½ teaspoon freshly ground black pepper

¼ teaspoon kosher salt

Vegan parm

2 tablespoons hemp hearts

1 tablespoon nutritional yeast

¼ teaspoon olive oil

⅛ teaspoon kosher salt

To assemble

4 cups washed salad greens or 1 (5-ounce) package salad greens

1. **Make the croutons:** In a large skillet, heat the oil over medium-high heat until shimmering. Add the chickpeas, salt, and pepper and fry, tossing occasionally, until the chickpeas are browned and crisp, about 8 minutes. Remove from skillet and drain on paper towels.

2. **Meanwhile, make the dressing:** In a food processor, combine the hummus, lemon juice, garlic, olive oil, mustard, tamari, capers, pepper, and salt and process until everything is fully incorporated into a thick dressing.

3. **Make the vegan parm:** In a small bowl, use clean hands to pinch together the hemp hearts, nutritional yeast, oil, and salt to make a crumbly cheese.

4. **Assemble the salad:** In a large bowl, toss the dressing with the salad greens. Arrange the dressed greens on a serving plate. Spoon the chickpeas over the greens. Sprinkle the parm over everything and serve immediately.

PLANT
This recipe is so vegan we even put it in the title.

PLANET
Get creative and swap in fresh, seasonal salad greens at peak freshness. Cook your own chickpeas for the hummus for a zero-waste boost!

NUTRITION, per serving

Calories: 644	Carbs: 69 g	Fiber: 20 g
Fat: 32 g	Protein: 26 g	Sugar: 13 g

Maitake Mushrooms with Spiced Yogurt

Serves 2

This is a dish that feels luxurious, yet only takes a few minutes to throw together—10 to be exact. Maitake, or hen of the woods, mushrooms can take some effort to find, but they're worth it. (Try a Korean or Japanese grocery if your farmers' market doesn't have them.) Layers of mushroom ruffles fry into crispy perfection after just a few minutes in oil. A spiced yogurt adds richness and a pecan crumble adds savory crunch. There's nothing like it.

Topping

¼ cup pecans, coarsely chopped

4 sprigs fresh thyme, leaves picked

½ garlic clove, grated

Kosher salt and freshly ground black pepper

Mushrooms

½ cup olive oil

2 maitake (hen of the woods) mushrooms, halved lengthwise

Kosher salt

Yogurt

½ cup plain yogurt of choice

1 tablespoon fresh lemon juice

1 teaspoon ras el hanout

¼ teaspoon kosher salt

1. **Make the topping:** In a large skillet, stir the pecans over medium-high heat as the skillet heats. When the skillet is hot and the pecans are fragrant, remove the pecans to a small bowl. Toss with the thyme, garlic, and salt and pepper to taste. Set aside.

2. **Make the mushrooms:** Wipe out the skillet and return to medium-high heat. Add the oil. When the oil is shimmering, gently lay the four mushroom halves in the skillet. Fry until crisp and browned on the bottom, about 2 minutes. Use tongs to carefully flip the mushrooms. Fry for 2 minutes more on the other side.

3. **Meanwhile, make the yogurt:** In a small bowl, mix together the yogurt, lemon juice, ras el hanout, and salt. Divide the yogurt mixture between two small serving plates.

4. When the mushrooms are finished, arrange two halves on each serving plate, on top of the yogurt. Season the mushrooms with a small pinch of salt. Sprinkle the pecan mixture over the top and serve immediately.

Note • Leftovers can be refrigerated for up to 1 week.

PLANT
This recipe can be made fully vegan.

PLANET
The yogurt mixture and crunchy topping can be repurposed for plenty of other grilled or roasted vegetables. Get creative!

NUTRITION, per serving, with ¼ cup olive oil

Calories: 423	Carbs: 19 g	Fiber: 6 g
Fat: 38 g	Protein: 8 g	Sugar: 8 g

10-Minute Curry

Curry is a dense and fascinating topic, its history shaped by colonialism and global diaspora, whose rich history deserves your study and attention. (While you're at it, google your entire spice rack for a better understanding of the flavors you've come to love.) In this instance, "curry" is used to mean curry powder mixed with a liquid and protein for a quick and satisfying meal. That's what this dish achieves in less than 10 minutes—and it's totally welcoming to the in-season, but perhaps slightly wilted, veggies in your fridge. Couscous acts as the base here—because time is of the essence—but any cooked grain you have on hand will have the same filling effect.

Couscous

1 cup couscous

¼ teaspoon kosher salt

Curry

2 tablespoons vegetable oil

1 small shallot, grated

2 garlic cloves, grated

1-inch piece fresh ginger, peeled and grated

1 tablespoon curry powder

½ teaspoon kosher salt

1 (15.5-ounce) can chickpeas, drained and rinsed, or 1½ cups cooked chickpeas or lentils (see Beans for Days, page 66), drained

¼ cup vegetable stock, store-bought or homemade (page 126)

1 cup plain yogurt of choice

Lime wedges and fresh cilantro leaves, for serving

1. **Make the couscous:** In a medium saucepan, bring 1 cup water to a boil over high heat. Remove from the heat, stir in the couscous and salt, and cover. Let the couscous sit for about 10 minutes, until the liquid is absorbed and the couscous is tender.

2. **Meanwhile, make the curry:** In a medium skillet, heat the oil over medium-high heat until shimmering. Add the shallot, garlic, ginger, and curry powder. Stir to coat in the oil and cook until the mixture is soft and fragrant, about 2 minutes. Add the salt, chickpeas, and vegetable stock. Stir to thoroughly coat in the seasoning, then simmer for about 2 minutes more until warmed through and fragrant. Remove from the heat and stir in the yogurt.

3. Divide the couscous among four bowls. Spoon the curry on top and serve with lime wedges and cilantro.

   Note • Store the couscous and curry in separate containers. Leftovers can be refrigerated for up to 1 week or frozen for up to 3 months.

PLANT
This recipe can be made fully vegan.

PLANET
Cook your own chickpeas or lentils to make this fully zero waste.

NUTRITION, per serving, without couscous

| Calories: 200 | Carbs: 22 g | Fiber: 5 g |
| Fat: 10 g | Protein: 8 g | Sugar: 8 g |

Vegan Cream of Tomato Soup

A quick, easy, dairy-free, and protein-packed shortcut to creamy soup might already be sitting in your fridge! Nope, it's not baby carrots, keep digging. It's hummus! Yes, hummus! Thrown in a blender with the usual suspects, it adds just the right amount of body-ody-ody and richness without overtaking the flavor. This recipe punches up the savory, warming flavors for a steaming tomato soup in under 10 minutes.

1 garlic clove, peeled

1 (28-ounce) can whole peeled tomatoes or 2 cups diced beefsteak tomatoes

1 (10-ounce) container hummus or 1¼ cups Use It Up Hummus (page 150)

1 cup vegetable stock, store-bought or homemade (page 126)

10 fresh basil leaves

1 tablespoon kosher salt

½ teaspoon tamari

¼ teaspoon red pepper flakes

1. In a blender, combine the garlic, tomatoes, hummus, stock, basil, salt, tamari, and pepper flakes. Blend on high until a smooth soup forms, about 2 minutes, scraping down the sides as needed. Transfer the soup to a large saucepan over medium-high heat. Simmer for about 5 minutes until fully warmed through.

2. Divide among four bowls and serve immediately.

Note • Leftovers can be refrigerated for up to 1 week or frozen for up to 3 months.

PLANT
This recipe is so vegan we even put it in the title.

PLANET
Fresh tomatoes are great in season, but canned will work beautifully year-round.

NUTRITION, per serving, with Use It Up Hummus

| Calories: 159 | Carbs: 19 g | Fiber: 7 g |
| Fat: 7 g | Protein: 8 g | Sugar: 6 g |

Mushroom Scallops with Quick Pea Mash

Serves 2

All the luxury of scallops, but with much less a) cost, b) environmental impact, c) stress about cooking. But definitely the same amount of speed! King trumpet mushrooms have the right density and texture to hold up to a quick fry. And in the time it takes them to brown, you can whip up a savory pea mash, too. It's a luxurious plant-based meal, ready in minutes.

3 king trumpet mushrooms, cleaned

2 tablespoons unsalted butter of choice

Kosher salt

½ cup fresh or frozen peas

1 tablespoon white miso

Juice of ½ lemon

Finely chopped fresh parsley, for serving

1. Cut the caps off the mushrooms and reserve for another use (like Vegetable Scrap Stock, page 126). Slice the stems of the mushrooms crosswise into 1-inch pieces, to resemble scallops.

2. In a medium skillet, melt the butter over medium-high heat and swirl to coat. Add the mushrooms in one even layer and sear until the bottoms are deeply browned, about 2 minutes. The butter will start to brown, too. Flip over the mushrooms and season with a generous pinch of salt. Add 1 tablespoon water to the skillet and cover. Continue to cook until the mushrooms are tender, about 4 minutes. Remove from the heat.

3. Meanwhile, in a small microwave-safe bowl, combine the peas and 1 tablespoon water. Microwave on high for 2 minutes, until the peas are hot. While the peas are in the microwave, add the miso and lemon juice to a food processor. Add the hot peas and process until a chunky mash forms, about 30 seconds.

4. Spoon the mash onto two plates and divide the mushroom scallops between the plates. Garnish with parsley and serve immediately.

Note • Leftovers can be refrigerated for up to 1 week.

PLANT
This recipe can be made fully vegan.

PLANET
Mushrooms and peas can be found at the farmers' market in the spring or fall months.

NUTRITION, per serving

| Calories: 192 | Carbs: 16 g | Fiber: 6 g |
| Fat: 13 g | Protein: 6 g | Sugar: 6 g |

Caramelized Banana & Orange Parfait

The height of smart luxury. Smart because everything here is good for you, luxury because in this particular combination it feels so indulgent. Bananas, chocolate, and walnuts give serious ice cream sundae vibes, while the orange, coconut, and yogurt keep things light and fun. And life skill alert: You'll learn how to supreme an orange, which will quickly be your new favorite technique for citrus fruit!

¼ cup walnuts or nut of choice, coarsely chopped

¼ cup unsweetened coconut flakes

1 cup Greek yogurt or yogurt of choice

2 teaspoons maple syrup

1 tablespoon refined coconut oil

1 large firm-ripe banana, sliced on the bias into ½-inch pieces

1 ounce dark chocolate, coarsely chopped

1 Cara Cara or Valencia orange, supremed (see sidebar, page 114)

1. In a medium skillet, toast the walnuts over medium-high heat, tossing the walnuts occasionally as the skillet heats up, about 2 minutes. Add the coconut flakes and toss to combine. Transfer the walnuts and coconut to a small bowl and set aside.

2. Meanwhile, in a small bowl, mix the yogurt and 1 teaspoon of the maple syrup and set aside.

3. Wipe out the skillet and return to medium-high heat. Add the oil and heat until shimmering. Add the banana slices in an even layer. Fry until golden brown on both sides and soft, about 2 minutes per side. Remove from the heat and drizzle the remaining 1 teaspoon maple syrup over the bananas. Set aside.

4. In a large glass, layer one-third of the yogurt mixture, half of the walnuts and coconut, and half of the chocolate. Make another layer with one-third of the yogurt, all of the orange segments, and the remaining chocolate. Add a final layer with the remaining yogurt, all of the bananas, and the remaining walnuts and coconut. Present the glass on a small plate with two spoons.

Note • Leftovers can be refrigerated for up to 1 week.

-recipe continues-

PLANT
This recipe can be made fully vegan.

PLANET
Be sure to buy maple syrup in a glass container that can be reused. Real maple syrup can be expensive, but grocery stores usually offer a variety of sizes to fit your budget.

NUTRITION, per serving

| Calories: 450 | Carbs: 40 g | Fiber: 6 g |
| Fat: 27 g | Protein: 16 g | Sugar: 27 g |

How to Supreme a Citrus Fruit

A perfectly peeled and segmented piece of citrus fruit is called a supreme (pronounced soo-PREM). No bitter pith, no strings, no membranes. You'll be reigning supreme in no time.

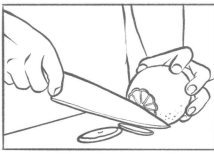

1. Cut a small slice from the top and the bottom of the citrus so you have a clear view of the fruit inside.

2. Set the citrus on one of the flat sides and run your knife from top to bottom, following the curve of the fruit, to remove the peel, white pith, and the enclosing membrane—but ideally not too much fruit. Rotate the fruit as you slice away small sections.

3. Hold the fruit over a bowl and carefully slide your knife in between the fruit and the white membrane to release the segments. Let the segments drop into the bowl along with all the delicious juice.

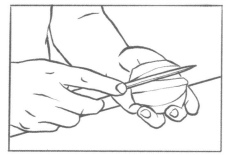

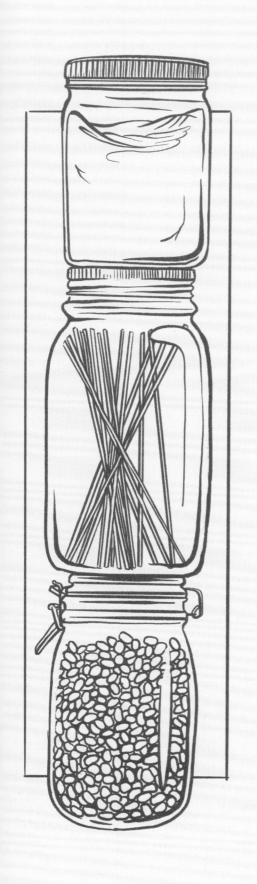

Lauren Singer

Environmental Activist &
Founder of Package Free

Before I jump into shopping for
food without waste, I'd love to
rewind to the beginning of my
journey to give you a better
understanding of why I live Zero
Waste. . . .

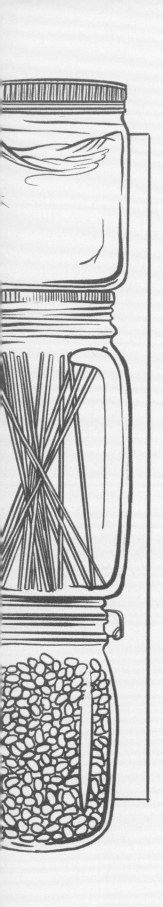

Back in 2012, I was studying environmental science at NYU and I spent much of my spare time protesting against fracking and big oil. A classmate of mine would bring take-out dinner to class and then throw away a plastic clamshell, plastic bag, and plastic utensils every day. I watched this happen over and over again, and one day I remember thinking, "How can you care about the environment while creating so much trash?" One night when making dinner, I opened my fridge and saw that I was doing the exact same thing: *everything* was packaged in plastic! It dawned on me that I wasn't living in alignment with my values; since most plastic is made from petroleum, I realized that my daily actions were subsidizing the very industry that I had been protesting against. That night I decided to change my consumption habits and eliminate excess plastic from my life.

Flash forward to nearly nine years later, it's safe to say that decision was the best one I have ever made for myself—and for the environment. Since then, I started a blog, *Trash Is for Tossers*, to share tips on reducing waste. I launched The Simply Co., a plastic-free, organic laundry detergent. I gave a TED Talk that raised awareness about Zero Waste. And I launched Package Free, a Zero Waste lifestyle store, to help make the world less trashy!

One of the most frequently asked questions I get is "How can I shop without waste?" It's an understandable concern. When you walk into a grocery store, it's not uncommon to feel completely surrounded by packaging. But I assure you, with a little bit of planning, you can reduce, or completely eliminate, waste from your grocery routine!

My biggest tip is to find a grocery store with a bulk section—most health food stores (like Whole Foods and smaller specialty stores) should have one. If not, don't fret! Just avoid plastic as best you can by opting for items packaged in easily recyclable materials, like paper, glass, and aluminum. Shopping at the farmers' market or sticking to the perimeter of the grocery store (which is where you'll usually find the fresh produce) is another way to steer clear of most processed, packaged foods. I always bring some essentials from Package Free with me: a few jars with lids for bulk items like pasta, grains, beans, and nut butter; some reusable bags to avoid using the thin, plastic produce ones, and a couple of totes to carry groceries home—**all sans plastic!**

Remember: You don't have to be fully Zero Waste to have a positive impact on the environment. Every small step, like saying "No, thank you" to a plastic bag at the store, is a positive one. With practice, reducing your waste can be easy, cost-effective, and fun!

Waste Not,
Want Not

Zero-waste recipes that use everything—skins, stems, and all—for a kitchen so sustainable even your compost bin will miss you.

Grainless Pie Crust with Whole-Citrus Filling

Serves 8

Place your mind somewhere between a frozen Key lime pie, a bitter Old Fashioned, and an orange smoothie. That's exactly where this pie lands. A simple nut/date/cocoa crust houses a pie made from an entire orange and an entire lemon (peels and all), blended into a sweet, tart, and smooth filling. It's a tangy, refreshing, frozen treat that couldn't be more summery.

Stewed citrus

1 medium navel orange

1 small lemon

¾ cup maple syrup

1 tablespoon agar-agar powder

Crust

1 tablespoon refined coconut oil, plus more for the pie plate

1½ cups walnuts

1 cup pitted Medjool dates (about 8)

3 tablespoons raw cacao powder

½ teaspoon kosher salt

Filling

½ cup maple syrup

16 ounces silken tofu

1 tablespoon finely chopped fresh rosemary

1 teaspoon vanilla extract

½ teaspoon kosher salt

1. **Stew the citrus:** Slice the stem ends off the orange and lemon. Halve the fruit and cut into ¼-inch slices, including the peels but discarding any seeds.

2. In a medium saucepan, combine the fruit, any accumulated juices, the maple syrup, and ½ cup water and bring to a simmer over medium heat. Reduce the heat to low and simmer until the fruit is falling off the rinds and the liquid is thick, 40 to 45 minutes. Remove the stewed fruit from the heat, sprinkle in the agar-agar, and stir to combine. Let the fruit and syrup cool for at least 5 minutes.

3. **Meanwhile, make the crust:** Rub a 9-inch pie plate with some coconut oil. Line with two 4-inch-wide strips of parchment paper in a crisscross, leaving a slight overhang on each side, and grease the paper with more oil.

4. In a food processor, combine the 1 tablespoon coconut oil, walnuts, dates, cacao powder, and salt and process until a crumbly mixture forms, about 1 minute, scraping down the sides as needed. Transfer the mixture into the prepared pie plate and press to the edges and about halfway up the sides, creating an even crust. Set aside.

–recipe continues–

5. **Make the filling:** In a blender, combine the maple syrup, tofu, rosemary, vanilla, and salt and blend on high for about 30 seconds to form a smooth mixture. When the stewed fruit has cooled, add it to the blender and blend on high until the rinds are fully incorporated into a pale orange mixture.

6. Pour the filling into the pie plate, reaching just over the crust. Smooth the filling with an offset spatula (or wet fingers!) before carefully transferring the pie to the freezer. Freeze for 4 hours, or make it a day ahead.

7. Thaw at room temperature for 15 minutes before lifting the pie out of the pie plate and slicing it into 8 wedges. Serve immediately. Any leftovers can be returned to the pie plate, covered with a piece of parchment paper to prevent frost, and refrozen immediately.

Note • Leftovers can be frozen for up to 2 months.

PLANT
This recipe is vegan.

PLANET
Navel oranges peak in the winter months, exactly when you need a reminder of summer.

NUTRITION, per serving

Calories: 421	Carbs: 66 g	Fiber: 5 g
Fat: 17 g	Protein: 8 g	Sugar: 54 g

Zero-Waste Pesto

Makes 2 cups

Pesto in the traditional *pesto alla genovese* sense is garlic, pine nuts, basil, and Parmesan. But what are rules for if not to be broken! This pesto uses walnuts, cheaper and more often in the pantry, plus a wide variety of greens in any combination. By using what you have, you're not only cutting back on waste, but you're also reinventing old dishes with bold new flavors. This recipe calls for nutritional yeast, but if cheese is in your diet, just swap in the same amount of grated Parmesan and cut the salt to ½ teaspoon.

6 cups greens in any combination (see chart)

1 cup walnuts

3 garlic cloves, peeled

¼ cup nutritional yeast

1 teaspoon kosher salt, plus more for seasoning

1 cup olive oil

1. Prepare the greens (see chart). Transfer the greens (and any cooked stems) to a food processor.

2. In a medium skillet (use the same skillet you used if you cooked any stems from the greens), toast the walnuts over medium heat, tossing occasionally, until warm and fragrant, about 2 minutes. Add the garlic with the walnuts if you want a softer garlic flavor.

3. Add the walnuts, garlic, yeast, and salt to the food processor. Process for about 30 seconds until the walnuts and greens are coarsely chopped. Add the oil and process for 10 to 20 seconds more until everything is incorporated into a chunky paste. (Don't process too long or the oil will turn bitter.) Taste for seasoning.

4. Pour into a container and refrigerate for up to 1 week.

Note • Pesto can be refrigerated for up to 1 week or portioned into smaller containers and frozen for up to 6 months.

PLANT
This recipe is vegan.

PLANET
Get creative and swap in fresh, seasonal produce.

NUTRITION, per ¼ cup, with spinach

Calories: 371	Carbs: 9 g	Fiber: 5 g
Fat: 36 g	Protein: 8 g	Sugar: 1 g

Greens	Notes
Arugula	All in!
Basil	Leaves and soft, tender stems
Beet greens	Leaves only; or, if you don't mind the color, stems cut into small pieces and cooked with a splash of water over medium heat
Broccoli	Tough outer layer of stalk peeled, head cut into small florets, and cooked with a splash of water over medium heat
Carrot tops	Stems and leaves
Chard	Leaves and stems (only use rainbow chard stems if you don't mind the color); stems cut into small pieces and cooked with a splash of water over medium heat
Cilantro	All in!
Kale	Leaves and stems; stems cut into small pieces and cooked with a splash of water over medium heat
Mint	Leaves and soft, tender stems
Parsley	Leaves and soft, tender stems
Spinach	All in!

Vegetable Scrap Stock

Makes 2 quarts

The easiest, best, and most beneficial way to cut back on waste in the kitchen is to recycle scraps into vegetable stock. (You'll consistently slice some $$$ off your grocery bill, too.) It's as easy as sliding your cutting board leftovers into a storage container and then taking a couple hours out of your day once or twice a month. Small investment, huge return!

1 tablespoon olive oil

4 cups frozen vegetable scraps in any combination (see chart)

2 medium pieces kombu, broken into coarse pieces

1 head garlic, halved horizontally

1 tablespoon whole black peppercorns

1. In a Dutch oven, heat the oil over medium-high heat. Add the vegetable scraps, kombu, garlic halves, and peppercorns. Cook, stirring occasionally, until the vegetables are thawed and the garlic is fragrant, 6 to 8 minutes.

2. Add 4 quarts cold water. Bring to a boil, then reduce the heat to low and simmer until the liquid is reduced by half, about 1 hour 30 minutes.

3. Set a large mesh sieve over a large bowl and drape a large tea towel over the sieve. Very slowly pour the broth into the tea towel, letting it drain through before adding more. Lift the sieve and tea towel out of the bowl and set over the Dutch oven. Use a potato masher to mash any remaining liquid gold from your scraps before discarding them. Pour the extra liquid into the bowl, then divide the broth between two 1-quart containers. (Remember to leave room for the liquid to expand as it freezes.) Keep one quart in the refrigerator to use within a week and keep the other in the freezer for up to 3 months.

Note • Keep a designated container in the freezer and add vegetable scraps as you cook. See the chart opposite for good scraps (all the perfect flavors) and bad scraps (too strong for stock). Vegetables that are on their way out can go in the container, but unfortunately mold is mold no matter how you freeze it; those scraps must be discarded.

PLANT
This recipe is vegan.

PLANET
This is a zero-waste recipe and the scraps are already paid for.

Good Scraps

Asparagus	Herb stems
Bell pepper	Leek
Carrot	Lettuce
Celery	Mushroom
Chard	Onion
Corn	Onion skin
Corn husk	Parsnip
Cucumber	Potato
Eggplant	Potato peel
Fennel	Scallion
Garlic	Shallot
Garlic skin	Spinach
Green bean	Squash
Herbs: basil, chives, cilantro, oregano, parsley, rosemary, thyme	Tomato
	Zucchini

Bad Scraps

Artichoke	Cauliflower
Beet	**Herbs:** dill, mint, sage
Bok choy	Radish
Broccoli	Rutabaga
Brussels sprouts	Turnip
Cabbage	

Whole-Veggie Burger

Veggie burgers come in a wide range of forms, from super-processed soy patties to barely-held-together objects that are more veggie than burger. This one achieves a perfect harmony of nutritious whole foods, lots of savory flavor, and enough natural binders to hold up like a burger should. Easy to fry, and just as easy to freeze for later, they're no waste and no worry!

1 small zucchini

1 medium carrot, scrubbed and unpeeled

1 small beet, scrubbed and unpeeled

1 cup dry-pack sun-dried tomatoes

2 garlic cloves, peeled

2 tablespoons onion powder (see Powders, page 225)

½ cup old-fashioned rolled oats

¼ cup almond flour or oat flour

2 tablespoons tamari

2 tablespoons white miso

1 tablespoon smoked paprika

1 teaspoon ground cumin

1 teaspoon kosher salt

½ teaspoon freshly ground black pepper

2 tablespoons vegetable oil, plus more as needed

Lettuce, sprouts, sliced buns, and Zero-Waste Pesto (page 124), for serving

1. Set the shredding disc in a food processor. Grate the zucchini, carrot, and beet and transfer to a bowl.

2. Change to the metal blade in the food processor. Add the sun-dried tomatoes, garlic, onion powder, oats, and almond flour. Process until the tomatoes and garlic are broken into coarse pieces. Add to the bowl with the vegetables.

3. Add the tamari, miso, smoked paprika, cumin, salt, and pepper to the bowl. Use clean hands to fully incorporate into a sticky mixture. Transfer to the refrigerator for 10 minutes.

4. In a medium skillet, heat the oil over medium heat. Remove the bowl from the refrigerator and divide the mixture into 4 patties, about 5 ounces each. When the oil is shimmering, lay two patties in the skillet and fry until golden brown on both sides, 2 to 3 minutes per side. Transfer to a plate and repeat with the remaining two patties, adding more oil to the skillet as needed.

5. Serve the burgers on buns with condiments of choice. (Alternatively, cool the cooked burgers and store in the refrigerator for up to 4 days or freezer for up to 3 months.)

PLANT
This recipe is vegan.

PLANET
Zucchini, beets, and carrots are all at their peak in the summer months, right when you need a burger the most.

NUTRITION, per serving

| Calories: 131 | Carbs: 11 g | Fiber: 3 g |
| Fat: 6 g | Protein: 4 g | Sugar: 6 g |

Zero-Waste Chips

Potato peel chips are the snack you didn't know you needed—and the snack you'll be making every time you peel spuds. Batch the spice mixes now to keep them at the ready. (They're also great for sprinkling on roasted veggies!) And when the craving strikes for a bigger, fuller crunch, don't worry: We show you how to make full potato chips, too.

Potato peel chips

Potato peels, in any amount

Vegetable oil or refined coconut oil

Salt or seasoning of choice (opposite)

1. Set a rack in the center of the oven and preheat to 425°F. Line a sheet pan with parchment paper.

2. Toss the peels in a small amount of oil (about ½ teaspoon per ¼ cup of peels). Spread in an even layer on the lined pan. Bake until they're browned and crispy, 15 to 20 minutes. Toss with a pinch of salt or seasoning of choice. Serve immediately.

Full potato chips

½ tablespoon vegetable oil or refined coconut oil, plus more for the pans

½ pound potatoes, scrubbed, unpeeled

Salt or seasoning of choice (opposite)

1. Set racks in the center and lower third of the oven and preheat to 425°F. Rub two sheet pans with a small amount of oil.

2. Cut the potatoes on a mandoline into slices about ⅛ inch thick. Toss with ½ tablespoon oil and spread in an even layer on the prepared baking sheets, leaving room between them.

3. Bake until they're browned and crispy, 15 to 20 minutes, rotating the sheets front to back halfway through. Toss with a pinch of salt or seasoning of choice. Serve hot.

Note • Leftovers can be stored in an airtight container at room temperature for up to 2 days.

PLANT
This recipe is vegan.

PLANET
Potatoes can be sustainably purchased year-round. The peel chips save on food waste and the full chips save on packaging. It's a smart move either way.

BBQ Seasoning · Makes ¼ cup

1 tablespoon kosher salt

1 tablespoon smoked paprika

½ tablespoon light brown sugar

½ tablespoon chili powder

½ tablespoon mustard powder

½ tablespoon garlic powder (see Powders, page 225)

½ tablespoon onion powder (see Powders, page 225)

In a screw-top jar, combine the salt, smoked paprika, brown sugar, chili powder, mustard powder, garlic powder, and onion powder and shake to combine. Store in a cool, dry place for up to 1 year.

Sour Cream & Onion Seasoning · Makes ½ cup

3 tablespoons buttermilk powder

2 tablespoons onion powder (see Powders, page 225)

1 tablespoon garlic powder (see Powders, page 225)

1 tablespoon kosher salt

½ tablespoon mustard powder

In a screw-top jar, combine the buttermilk powder, onion powder, garlic powder, salt, and mustard powder and shake to combine. Store in a cool, dry place for up to 1 year.

NUTRITION, Zero-Waste Chips, per ¼ pound

Calories: 135	Carbs: 24 g	Fiber: 2 g
Fat: 4 g	Protein: 3 g	Sugar: 1 g

NUTRITION, BBQ Seasoning, per ½ tablespoon

Calories: 11	Carbs: 2 g	Fiber: 1 g
Fat: 0 g	Protein: 0 g	Sugar: 1 g

NUTRITION, Sour Cream & Onion Seasoning, per ½ tablespoon

Calories: 12	Carbs: 2 g	Fiber: 0 g
Fat: 0 g	Protein: 1 g	Sugar: 1 g

Seedy Crackers with Whole-Beet Dip

Serves 4

These crackers are free of allergens and fully customizable to what's in your pantry. The fact that they're also zero waste only makes them better. While the crackers bake, why not waste even less by throwing together a quick beet dip that uses the full vegetable? (Use It Up Hummus, page 150, is also a great option!) Cutting back never tasted so good.

Crackers

1 cup flaxseed meal

1 cup assorted seeds, such as pumpkin, sunflower, chia, sesame, hemp, and poppy

½ garlic clove, minced

2 teaspoons finely chopped fresh rosemary or 1 teaspoon dried rosemary

1 teaspoon kosher salt

1 teaspoon freshly ground black pepper

Refined coconut oil

Pesto and dip

1 medium beet, scrubbed, stem and leaves separated, and everything cut into 1-inch pieces

¼ cup plus 2 tablespoons olive oil

1 tablespoon white wine vinegar

Kosher salt

½ cup cooked chickpeas (see Beans for Days, page 66)

¼ cup tahini

½ garlic clove

¼ teaspoon freshly ground black pepper

1. Set a rack in the center of the oven and preheat to 350°F. Line a sheet pan with parchment paper.

2. **Make the crackers:** In a large bowl, mix the flaxseed meal, seeds, garlic, rosemary, salt, and pepper. Add 1 cup water and stir to fully incorporate. Let the mixture sit for about 10 minutes to hydrate.

3. Turn the mixture out onto the lined sheet pan. Brush another piece of parchment with coconut oil and place on top of the mixture. Use a rolling pin to roll into a 14 × 8-inch rectangle. Lift the parchment and use hands dipped in oil to help shape the dough as you roll it out. (It's okay if the corners are slightly rounded.)

4. Use a pizza cutter or large knife to cut lengthwise into 4 strips. Rotate the baking sheet and make 8 evenly spaced cuts across to make 9 strips, or 36 crackers total. Bake until the crackers are golden brown and crisp, 50 to 60 minutes. Cool completely on the pan.

5. **Meanwhile, make the pesto:** In a food processor, combine the beet greens, 2 tablespoons of the oil, the vinegar, and a large pinch of salt and pulse 3 or 4 times to make a coarsely chopped pesto. Transfer the beet green pesto to a small bowl, cover, and refrigerate.

–recipe continues–

6. **Make the dip:** Add the beet (the peel can stay on the beet for added nutrition) and stem to the same food processor (it's okay for the remnants from the pesto to get mixed in here). Process for 30 seconds to 1 minute until the beet is coarsely chopped.

7. In a large skillet, heat the remaining ¼ cup oil over medium heat until shimmering. Add the beet and stem and cook, stirring occasionally, until everything is softened, about 5 minutes.

8. Meanwhile, add the chickpeas, tahini, garlic, ½ teaspoon salt, and the pepper to the food processor. Add the beets, stems, and all the oil from the skillet. Process until a smooth dip forms, about 1 minute, scraping down the sides as needed. Depending on the size of the beet, the mixture might be too thick, so add water 1 tablespoon at a time to help blend. Transfer the dip to a medium bowl, cover, and refrigerate.

9. When the crackers are cooled, spoon some of the beet greens pesto on top and serve with the dip.

Note • Eat it right away. Alternatively, refrigerate the dip for up to 1 week and store the crackers in an airtight container at room temperature for up to 3 days.

PLANT
This recipe is vegan.

PLANET
Beets can be found at the farmers' market in the summer, fall, or winter months. Everything else might be sitting in your pantry already.

NUTRITION, Crackers, per serving

| Calories: 318 | Carbs: 18 g | Fiber: 13 g |
| Fat: 24 g | Protein: 12 g | Sugar: 1 g |

NUTRITION, Whole Beet Dip, per serving

| Calories: 271 | Carbs: 15 g | Fiber: 4 g |
| Fat: 22 g | Protein: 6 g | Sugar: 5 g |

Stuffed Mushrooms

Serves 6 to 10

Hot take, but stuffed mushrooms are kind of the best mushrooms. Bursting with juicy mushroom flavor, stuffed with a savory filling, and finished with an herby topping, they just hit different. Bonus: These mushrooms are covered in toasted nuts for a savory crunch in every bite. Pro tip: Make a tray now and toss them into salads throughout the week.

2 tablespoons plus 1 teaspoon olive oil

¾ cup walnuts or pecans

6 sprigs fresh parsley, stems and leaves, cut into ½-inch pieces

1 pound baby bella (cremini) mushrooms

½ teaspoon kosher salt, plus more for seasoning

¼ teaspoon freshly ground black pepper, plus more for seasoning

1 garlic clove, peeled

2 ounces feta cheese, broken into small chunks

1. Set a rack in the center of the oven and preheat to 400°F. Rub 1 tablespoon of the oil on a sheet pan.

2. In a food processor, combine the walnuts and 2 of the parsley sprigs and pulse 3 or 4 times until the nuts and parsley are in coarse pieces. Transfer the walnut mixture to a small bowl and set aside.

3. Remove the stems from the mushroom caps. Place the stems in the same food processor (it's okay if a little pecan mixture gets in the mushroom filling) along with any mushrooms too small to stuff or too hard to stem.

4. Place the caps in a medium bowl and add 1 tablespoon of the oil, the salt, and pepper and toss to combine. Arrange the caps on the prepared baking sheet. Set aside.

5. Add the garlic and remaining 4 parsley sprigs to the food processor with the mushroom stems. Pulse 6 to 8 times until everything is broken down into small pieces. Add the feta and pulse 3 or 4 more times to combine into a cohesive filling. Use a small spoon to fill each cap with a rounded mound of filling.

6. Add the remaining 1 teaspoon oil, a pinch of salt, and a few grinds of pepper to the bowl with the walnut mixture. Lift a stuffed mushroom (careful, it'll be slippery!) and dip the filling side into the walnut mixture. Press down gently to flatten and coat the filling in the nuts. Return the mushroom to the baking sheet and repeat with the remaining mushrooms.

7. Bake the mushrooms until the walnuts are golden and the mushrooms are cooked, 15 to 20 minutes. Transfer to a serving platter and serve immediately.

Note • Eat it right away. Alternatively, refrigerate the stuffed mushrooms and pecan topping separately for up to 1 week. Dip and bake the mushrooms as needed.

PLANT
This recipe is vegetarian, but swap in vegan cheese to make it fully plant-based.

PLANET
Mushrooms can be found at the farmers' market in the spring and fall months. Everything else might be sitting in your pantry already.

NUTRITION, per serving, based on 10 servings

Calories: 179	Carbs: 6 g	Fiber: 3 g
Fat: 16 g	Protein: 5 g	Sugar: 3 g

Zucchini & Cashew Soup

This soup has a short ingredient list and is ready in under 30 minutes, but don't be fooled. The density, creaminess, and complexity make it taste like a multistep all-day affair. Because it's so simple, it's important to use the very best ingredients. You're going to use the whole vegetable—stem and all—so freshly picked zucchini will elevate this in ways grocery store zucchini just can't.

2 pounds zucchini, washed

1 cup raw cashews

4 cups vegetable stock, store-bought or homemade (page 126)

1 tablespoon olive oil

2 teaspoons kosher salt

1 teaspoon freshly ground black pepper

2 tablespoons dried herbs (see Dehydrating, page 224), like parsley, chives, or dill, or ground spices (see Powders, page 225), like garlic, onion, or chili powder, in any combination (optional)

1. Chop the zucchini into 2-inch chunks, leaving the stem intact. In a large saucepan, combine the zucchini, cashews, vegetable stock, olive oil, salt, pepper, and any herbs or spices (if using). Bring to a boil over high heat. Reduce the heat to medium and simmer until the zucchini is soft and the cashews are swollen, about 20 minutes.

2. Carefully pour the soup into a blender. Open the steam vent in the lid, hold a folded kitchen towel over the hole, and blend on high for 1 to 2 minutes until the soup is smooth and fully combined.

3. Divide among four bowls and serve warm.

Note • Leftovers can be refrigerated for up to 1 week or frozen for up to 3 months. The soup is great served hot or chilled.

PLANT
This recipe is vegan.

PLANET
Zucchini is at its peak freshness in the summer months. Everything else might be sitting in your pantry already.

NUTRITION, per serving

Calories: 258	Carbs: 18 g	Fiber: 3 g
Fat: 19 g	Protein: 9 g	Sugar: 7 g

Nadiya Hussain

Chef, Author &
Television Host

It is the boring bit, but we must start with the stats that leave us floored, jaws on the ground, but with all the will in the world to change. According to the United States Department of Agriculture, an average of just less than 10 percent of disposable income

is spent on food. The divide is almost split right down the middle, with half being spent on groceries and the other half on dining out. Even then, the average American throws away about 238 pounds of food each year!

What does 238 pounds look like? It looks like a grizzly bear, a brown bear, a monk seal, a gazelle. If neither the weight nor the comparison to large animals means anything, it is a lot of food to waste! If you start with 238 pounds per person and multiply by America's population of more than 300 million people . . . that is a lot of waste. But waste can be avoided, one person, one family, at a time.

First we have to be rid of the notion of "How can my changes, as one person, help?" because small steps can absolutely make a difference. If we all adopt a different way of approaching food, waste, and spending habits, we can make big changes over time. Living sustainably does not mean we have to transform into a domestic divinity who has hours to spare to make everything from scratch. We live in modern times, at a fast pace, constantly pressed for time. Food can fall by the wayside, but it does not have to.

Take it from a woman who worked three jobs just to pay the bills as a youth, and now is still juggling multiple careers as a TV host, writer, and cook, plus a homemaker with three kids: We have to use our money wisely rather than making it work relentlessly!

A few simple habits I have adopted:

1. Keep a shopping list on your phone to write what you need when you realize you need it, then delete it after you buy it.

2. Don't make whimsical trips to the store. That is your mind telling you that you need things you really don't and you will no doubt end up buying things you neither need nor want, which leads right to waste.

3. Meal prep! I have a standard three-week rotation of meals. This keeps it exciting because the pad Thai my family loved tonight will be right there for dinner in three weeks. It takes the thinking out of it for you, while keeping the variety alive. Having meal plans means you know what you need and can really direct your movement when shopping. No distractions.

4. Eat out less and only when it is a special occasion. Eating out is expensive and is less meaningful when you are eating out every time you do not feel like making dinner.

5. Think about what you are buying and when you are buying them. You can't buy a month's worth of fresh ingredients and expect it to keep, so . . .

6. Buy food with a long shelf life, like pasta, dried beans, spices, and condiments. They will keep and they are worth stocking up on. And don't forget canned foods. *Canned* is not a bad word: Often beans and lentils take hours to soak and precook, so a can will save you both money and time.

7. Buy your perishables, like eggs, cheese, and vegetables, every week, based on your weekly menu.

8. Biggest one of all: Utilize your appliances! You can use your microwave and oven to dry up wilted old herbs, while your freezer can store almost anything from nuts to bread to soft fruit.

Saving food saves money! For our pockets and the planet, waste is not okay. Small steps by just one person or one family make a difference. Every practice, no matter how small, is closer to living a more sustainable life.

Clear
Out

Dying produce, a crowded pantry,
an overextended freezer?
We have solutions!

Pantry Fagioli

An easy and satisfying soup is probably already in your kitchen. *Pasta e fagioli* started its life as a peasant dish, meaning people used what they had on hand. A quick raid of the pantry and freezer, a few minutes over the stove, and suddenly you have something warm, hearty, and brothy that hits the spot.

2 tablespoons olive oil

1 medium yellow onion, finely chopped

2 garlic cloves, minced

Kosher salt and freshly ground black pepper

1 teaspoon dried oregano

1 (1-pound) bag frozen mixed vegetables or 3¾ cups of finely chopped mixed fresh vegetables

4 cups vegetable stock, store-bought or homemade (page 126)

1 (28-ounce) can diced tomatoes or 2 cups diced beefsteak tomatoes

1 (15.5-ounce) can Great Northern beans, drained and rinsed, or 1¾ cups cooked Great Northern beans (see Beans for Days, page 66), drained

2 cups uncooked ditalini or small pasta shape or 2 cups cooked grains (see Grains for the Week, page 64)

Zero-Waste Pesto (see page 124), for serving (optional)

1. In a Dutch oven or large soup pot, heat the oil over medium heat until shimmering. Add the onion and garlic, season generously with salt and pepper, and cook, stirring occasionally, until the onion is soft and the garlic is fragrant, about 10 minutes. Add the oregano and cook for about 1 more minute, until the oregano is fragrant.

2. Add the vegetables and cook until slightly thawed (or slightly tender if using fresh vegetables), about 2 minutes. Add the vegetable stock, increase the heat to medium-high, and bring to a boil. Add the tomatoes, beans, and pasta (if using cooked grains, add later) and stir to combine. Cover, reduce the heat to low, and simmer until the pasta is al dente, 6 to 8 minutes. (If using cooked grains, add now and simmer for about 1 minute until warmed through.)

3. Remove the soup from the heat and taste for seasoning. Portion into bowls and serve immediately with a generous scoop of pesto (if using).

Note • Leftovers can be refrigerated for up to 1 week or frozen for up to 3 months.

PLANT
This recipe is vegan.

PLANET
The vegetables are fully interchangeable, so use what's currently in season or save dying vegetables to cut back on packaging.

NUTRITION, per serving

| Calories: 164 | Carbs: 26 g | Fiber: 4 g |
| Fat: 4 g | Protein: 6 g | Sugar: 3 g |

Black Bean & Walnut Quesadillas

The powerhouse combo of black beans and walnuts is a perfect marriage of protein and texture, providing a dense, satisfying bite. A smooth and spicy cheese sauce adds a delightful richness and tons of flavor. (If dairy is in your diet, go ahead and substitute shredded cheese!) Perfectly flexible; use any wilting greens that need to go, like, now. And packed into a warm, toasted tortilla? Wow. There's just nothing like a quesadilla.

1 tablespoon olive oil

1 cup raw walnuts, finely chopped

½ teaspoon dried oregano

¼ teaspoon chili powder

1 (15.5-ounce) can black beans, drained and rinsed, or 1½ cups cooked black beans (see Beans for Days, page 66)

2 cups roughly chopped spinach, kale, or chard

½ teaspoon kosher salt

2 (9-inch) flour tortillas

Vegan Cheese Sauce (recipe follows) or 2 cups shredded cheese

1. In a medium skillet, heat the oil over medium heat until shimmering. Add the walnuts, oregano, and chili powder and cook, stirring occasionally, until the walnuts are toasted and fragrant, about 2 minutes. Add the black beans, spinach, and salt. Cook, stirring occasionally, until the spinach is wilted and the black beans are warmed through, about 4 minutes more. Transfer to a medium bowl and set aside. Wipe out the skillet.

2. Return the skillet to medium heat. Lay a tortilla in the skillet and spread half of the walnut filling on one side of the tortilla, leaving room at the edge. Drizzle about ½ cup of the cheese sauce (or 1 cup of shredded cheese) over the filling and fold the tortilla in half. Cook for about 3 minutes until the bottom is toasted, then flip and cook for about 3 minutes more to toast the other side. Transfer to a cutting board and repeat with the remaining tortilla, filling, and cheese sauce. Cut the quesadillas in quarters and serve immediately.

Note • Leftovers can be refrigerated for up to 1 week.

Vegan Cheese Sauce · Makes 1 cup

1 cup raw cashews

½ cup boiling water

⅓ cup nutritional yeast

1 garlic clove, smashed

1 jalapeño, halved and seeded

¼ cup olive oil

¾ teaspoon kosher salt

½ teaspoon smoked paprika

½ teaspoon chili powder

½ teaspoon ground cumin

1. In a blender, combine the cashews, boiling water, nutritional yeast, garlic, jalapeño, oil, salt, smoked paprika, chili powder, and cumin. Let soak in the blender jar for 30 minutes.

2. Blend the mixture on high until a smooth sauce forms, about 1 minute, scraping down the sides as needed. (Store the cheese sauce in the refrigerator for up to 1 week.)

PLANT
This recipe is vegan.

PLANET
Spinach is in season during the spring and fall months, but kale and chard can take over in the other seasons.

NUTRITION, per serving

Calories: 739	Carbs: 53 g	Fiber: 16 g
Fat: 51 g	Protein: 26 g	Sugar: 3 g

Use It Up Hummus

Hummus is always a smart idea. Great for snacking, sandwiches, salads, or soups (see Vegan Cream of Tomato Soup, page 109), it should always be in your fridge. But cut the grocery bill and save the plastic by getting in the habit of making your own. Once you have the standard recipe down, feel free to start playing around, adding olives, roasted peppers, herbs, and spices as your imagination sees fit.

1 (15.5-ounce) can chickpeas, drained and rinsed, or 1½ cups cooked chickpeas (see Beans for Days, page 66)

¾ cup tahini

½ cup olive oil

1 garlic clove, peeled

Juice of 1 lemon

1 teaspoon kosher salt

Any toppings, like olives, roasted vegetables, herbs, and spices (optional)

1. In a food processor, combine the chickpeas, tahini, oil, garlic, lemon juice, salt, and 2 tablespoons water. Process until a thick paste forms, about 2 minutes, scraping down the sides as needed. Taste for seasoning and add water 1 tablespoon at a time to adjust the thickness.

2. Transfer the mixture to a serving bowl. Top with any desired toppings and serve immediately.

Note • Leftovers can be refrigerated for up to 1 week.

PLANT
This recipe is vegan.

PLANET
Everything in this recipe can be sustainably purchased year-round and might even be sitting in your pantry already.

NUTRITION, per ¼ cup

| Calories: 273 | Carbs: 16 g | Fiber: 4 g |
| Fat: 21 g | Protein: 7 g | Sugar: 2 g |

Baked Oatmeal with Frozen Fruit

A great meal-prep breakfast or brunch for a crowd that won't require a trip to the store. What could be easier! Baked oatmeal takes on a perfectly tender bite while the banana, maple syrup, and fruit add a nice background sweetness. If you're feeling extra sweet, go ahead and drizzle on a little more syrup. No one will judge you.

2 tablespoons cold unsalted butter of choice, cubed, plus 1 tablespoon, softened, for the baking pan

1 medium banana, mashed

2 large eggs

2 cups old-fashioned rolled oats

1 cup milk of choice

¼ cup maple syrup, plus more for serving

1 teaspoon ground cinnamon

1 teaspoon baking powder

½ teaspoon kosher salt

2 cups frozen fruit

1. Set a rack in the center of the oven and preheat to 350°F. Coat an 8 × 8-inch baking pan with the softened butter.

2. In a large bowl, whisk together the banana and eggs. Add the oats, milk, maple syrup, cinnamon, baking powder, and salt and whisk to combine. Use a spatula to fold in the frozen fruit and then transfer the oatmeal to the prepared baking pan. Dot the butter cubes over the top.

3. Bake until the oatmeal is set and golden brown, 45 to 50 minutes. Cool in the pan for 20 minutes before slicing into 6 pieces and serving.

Note • Leftovers can be refrigerated for up to 1 week.

PLANT
This recipe is vegetarian.

PLANET
Fresh fruit can be substituted, of course, but frozen fruit makes this a breakfast staple year-round. Freeze your own fruit in the summer months for year-round sustainability.

NUTRITION, per serving

| Calories: 346 | Carbs: 30 g | Fiber: 2 g |
| Fat: 7 g | Protein: 4 g | Sugar: 23 g |

Chickpea Tuna Salad

An old favorite in plant-based diets—because canned tuna is a famously bad choice for fish everywhere—the chickpea tuna salad is the perfect answer to any number of questions. What should I bring? What should I snack on? What do I want for lunch this week? If you don't have dill lying around, just swap in parsley or chives. Or use half the amount of dried herbs. Or skip the herbs altogether. It's your dish!

1 (15.5-ounce) can chickpeas, drained and rinsed, or 1½ cups cooked chickpeas (see Beans for Days, page 66)

1 garlic clove, grated

Juice of ½ lemon

½ small red onion, finely chopped

2 tablespoons plain yogurt of choice or mayonnaise of choice

2 tablespoons hemp hearts

1 tablespoon capers, drained and coarsely chopped

1 tablespoon tamari

1 sheet nori, thinly sliced

1 tablespoon finely chopped fresh dill

Toasted bread or crackers (see page 133), for serving

1. In a medium bowl, combine the chickpeas, garlic, lemon juice, onion, yogurt, hemp hearts, capers, and tamari and stir together with a wooden spoon. Use the back of the spoon to mash about half of the chickpeas. Stir in the nori and dill.

2. Pile the salad onto slices of toasted bread or serve in a bowl alongside crackers.

   Note • Leftovers can be refrigerated for up to 1 week.

PLANT
This recipe is vegan.

PLANET
Everything in this recipe can be sustainably purchased year-round. Cook your own chickpeas to make this even more zero waste.

NUTRITION, per serving

Calories: 157	Carbs: 22 g	Fiber: 5 g
Fat: 4 g	Protein: 9 g	Sugar: 4 g

Spicy Braised Cabbage

Serves 4

We've all been here: You had to buy an entire head of cabbage for a few shreds on a taco and you're left wondering . . . what's next? Hi, hello. Here's the answer. Dense and spicy but not heavy, this is cabbage like you've never seen her before. It's a perfect side dish to any meal or the centerpiece to a harvest dinner.

Leftover head of cabbage, red or green (about 2 pounds)

1 tablespoon plus 1 teaspoon kosher salt, plus more as needed

4 tablespoons olive oil

2 garlic cloves, thinly sliced

¼ cup gochujang

2 tablespoons tamari

2 tablespoons coconut sugar or sugar of choice

1 (14.5-ounce) can diced tomatoes or 1¾ cups diced beefsteak tomatoes

Fresh herbs, such as parsley, cilantro, basil, or fennel fronds, roughly chopped, for serving

1. Cut the cabbage into four even wedges. (Or as close as possible, working with what you have left.) Thoroughly salt the cabbage with 1 tablespoon of the salt (or more as needed), rubbing it into the crevices. Set the cabbage quarters on a wire rack set over a sheet pan. Allow the cabbage to sweat for 1 hour.

2. Set a rack in the center of the oven and preheat to 400°F.

3. In a cast-iron skillet, heat 2 tablespoons of the oil over medium-high heat until shimmering. Add two of the cabbage quarters, cut-side down. Sear for about 5 minutes until deeply charred, then flip and sear the other side for about 5 minutes more. Remove the quarters to the wire rack. Add the remaining 2 tablespoons oil and repeat the same process with the remaining two quarters. Remove the cabbage and set aside.

4. Reduce the heat to medium-low and add the garlic, gochujang, tamari, and coconut sugar to the skillet. Cook, stirring often, until the gochujang is softened and the sugar is dissolved, about 1 minute. Add the tomatoes and stir to combine. Once the mixture begins to simmer, arrange the cabbage quarters in the skillet and pour in 1 cup water.

5. Transfer to the oven and bake until the cabbage is falling-apart tender and the sauce is thick, 50 minutes to 1 hour. Blanket with herbs and serve immediately.

Note • Leftovers can be refrigerated for up to 1 week.

PLANT
This recipe is vegan.

PLANET
Cabbage can be found at the farmers' market in the summer, fall, and winter months. Everything else might be sitting in your pantry already.

NUTRITION, per serving

| Calories: 446 | Carbs: 73 g | Fiber: 17 g |
| Fat: 16 g | Protein: 14 g | Sugar: 49 g |

Anything Salad

"Where's the recipe?!" you ask. "In your fridge," we reply. A salad can be literally anything, but sometimes an instruction to "eyeball it" can send the best intentions right off the rails. So here is an easy formula to follow, with plenty of room to be flexible with what you have. Some ideas are listed below, but feel free to experiment, combine, and make mistakes. In other words, play with your food!

¼ cup nuts or seeds in any combination

½ cup dressing of any kind (see Dressings, page 220)

2 cups (5 ounces) salad greens in any combination, washed and dried

1 cup chopped raw or roasted vegetables (see Roasting Veggies, page 68) in any combination

½ cup fresh herb leaves in any combination (see chart)

¼ cup pickled vegetables (see Pickles, page 213) in any combination, drained and coarsely chopped

Kosher salt and freshly ground black pepper

1. In a small skillet, toast the nuts or seeds over medium heat, tossing occasionally as the skillet heats up, until everything is warm and fragrant, 2 to 5 minutes. Transfer to a small bowl and stir in 2 tablespoons of the dressing. Set aside.

2. Add ¼ cup of the dressing to the bottom of a large bowl with plenty of room for tossing. Add the greens and use clean hands to gently toss, lifting from the bottom up to incorporate the dressing. Add the vegetables, herbs, pickles, dressed nuts, a good pinch of salt, and plenty of black pepper. Toss again and taste for dressing and seasoning. A salad often needs more salt and pepper rather than more dressing, but add the remaining 2 tablespoons dressing if it needs it.

3. Divide the salad between two bowls and serve immediately.

   Note • Eat it right away. Dressed salad doesn't store well.

Nuts/Seeds	Dressing	Greens	Vegetable	Herb	Pickle
Pistachio, chopped	Avocado ranch	Kale	Roasted potatoes	Dill	Beets
Sunflower	Lemon and olive oil	Arugula	Sliced radish	Basil	Fennel
Walnut	Balsamic vinaigrette	Romaine	Roasted carrots	Mint	Red onion

PLANT
This recipe is vegan.

PLANET
Get creative and swap in fresh, seasonal produce. Everything else might be sitting in your pantry already.

NUTRITION, per serving, without dressing and with walnuts, roasted sweet potato, and salad greens

Calories: 206	Carbs: 27 g	Fiber: 8 g
Fat: 9 g	Protein: 7 g	Sugar: 6 g

Kelis Rogers

Musician, Chef & Farmer

What do I know about farming? Very little, to be honest. We have all heard terms like *sustainability*, *carbon footprint*, *eco-friendly*, *holistic*, *farm-to-table*, *homesteading*, *ethical consumerism*, *fair trade*, *foraging*, and *forest stewardship* thrown around. A few years ago, these were all new terms to me and I would be lying if I said they excited me at all. They always seemed daunting and style prohibitive, which I just wasn't into.

So the question is, how did I get here? Here being living on a farm with two cows, four goats, six sheep, twenty-one chickens, three dogs, four cats, and a partridge in a pear tree. Coming from the concrete jungle, New York City, and moving to Los Angeles, California, I felt like I was selling myself short. This giant suburb was not a city and it certainly wasn't country living either. But ironically that's where the idea of living a healthier life began.

These fleeting thoughts over the course of a few busy years would pop into view. Like we used to have these neighbors—friends, really—that right next door would grow the most gorgeous tomatoes and even corn! I loved when we got the brown paper bag of their fresh produce, then my heart would sink. I don't have a green thumb and I've always had an easier time killing plants than keeping them alive. But I kept feeling like surely if they could do it, I could at least try. So one day, I bought one of those little herb aquaponics kits that you plug in on the kitchen counter. The idea of digging dirt and planting just seemed so far away for me at the time, and it was certainly a commitment that I was not quite ready for. So I started small, with this little herb box in my house.

Like most things in life, gardening (and farming) starts with a small idea. So how can we begin? What can each of us individually do, in a realistic way, that will allow us to make a collective impact? I believe it's unrealistic to expect or even ask people to change who they are. I know I won't change. But I think as we know more, we do more. So instead of going to the grocery store and buying anonymously, I look to farms and farmers' markets in my area, local people I can go visit and talk to and learn from. They need us as much as we need them. So let's stop ignoring one another! Small farmers

are able to meet us where we are with delivery services or CSAs. They give back and offer you control over your food. It's an easy start for anyone.

I obviously took it a step further, or like 600,000 steps further, when I bought sheep and goats. (They are nature's lawn mower and weed trimmer in one.) But as a chef and farmer, I'm always trying to minimize food waste, using a rooter-to-tooter mentality with my produce, maximizing every ingredient, using everything, finding value in otherwise forgotten produce. I think our first most valuable step in the right direction is reconnection, rethinking what we actually want and expect from our lives. On a really basic level. Not overly existential deep thoughts. I'm talking about the real stuff. I want to be healthy, but what is healthy to me? How do I share that with my kids so they can form habits they can sustain and use?

"Let's eat better" is an easy thing to say. But how do you do that? It calls for a little quality control. Think about what you need and what you and your family like to eat. What is in season? How can you support the farms nearest to you so they can keep the treats coming your way? Or how can you start the growing process yourself? And again, it's the small step. Get a pot, find some sunshine, a windowsill or patio if you have one, grab some great potting soil, a few like-minded herbs (pro tip: sage, thyme, and rosemary are really good friends), a splash of water, a lot of love, and you're off!

Here at the farm, we've been learning about composting. I mean super-base-level stuff. Right now, it seems to be a big smelly heap that we are supposed to keep flipping and wetting and I let my husband play with that. But even composting can come down to earth (pun intended) with a small step. Like when you eat a banana, stick it in a jar with water and let it sit for two days. Pour that liquid gold all over your plants. It's got phosphorus, potassium, and calcium, which help make the plants more resistant to pests. Or save your morning coffee grounds and eggshells. Add those scraps to your plants as a natural fertilizer. It's the simple things that you suddenly see differently, the trash that now gives your garden superpowers. These are the small steps that can work for anyone—whether you're in a New York City apartment, a farm in Southern California, or somewhere in between—all helping to lead you into a more sustainable and healthy way of life.

Something else I've started to think about is how much more can our food serve us. What should it be able to do? I have two deliciously hilarious, lovable boys. My world consists of superheroes and intense debates on worthy superpowers and weapons. To get them excited about eating their vegetables, nature's original superpowers, they've grown up hearing me say things like "Eat all your broccolini, it will make you run faster!" or "Try these carrots, don't you want X-ray vision?" So now whether we are in the garden or at the dinner table, my little one will say, "But, Mama, what will it do?!" He means what powers will he get for eating this vegetable. It never gets old and makes me laugh every time. But isn't that how we all should be thinking? What can this give me to sustain my mind and body?

It can all be overwhelming; trust me, I know. So, it's really just about taking one step at a time. Figuring out what works best for you. Some home gardening? Weekly farmers' market visits? Composting? One tiny decision, one after another, toward better health for oneself, our community, and our planet, and all the residual effects spill out from there. As my mom used to say, in her most matter-of-fact way, "Well, when you know better, you do better." So, let's all try to do better.

These recipes score high on sustainability, compromise a bit on "healthy," and fly off the charts on fun.

Date & Tahini Fruit Crisp

Beautiful fruit at the height of its season deserves the gentlest touch possible. This dessert sits in the perfect place of not-too-sweet with lots of supportive savory flavors to lift up the real star of the dish: the fruit. One cup of sesame seeds might seem like a lot—hello, bulk bin!—but after one bite of a perfectly crisp topping, it'll all make sense. Swap out the fruit with each season and discover this dessert over and over.

Fruit

2 pounds fruit, peeled, pitted, trimmed, and sliced, as needed

½ cup packed light brown sugar

1 tablespoon ground cinnamon

1 teaspoon kosher salt

1 teaspoon cornstarch

Crisp

10 pitted dates, finely chopped

½ cup maple syrup

⅔ cup tahini

2 tablespoons refined coconut oil

2 cups old-fashioned rolled oats

1 cup sesame seeds

1 tablespoon ground cinnamon

2 teaspoons kosher salt

Whipped cream or ice cream, for serving

1. Set a rack in the center of the oven and preheat to 375°F.

2. **Prepare the fruit:** In a 9 × 13-inch baking pan, toss the fruit, sugar, cinnamon, salt, and cornstarch. Set aside.

3. **Prepare the crisp:** In a medium saucepan, bring the dates and maple syrup to a boil over medium heat. Let the maple syrup continue to boil until reduced and thickly coating the dates, about 5 minutes. Remove from the heat and stir in the tahini and coconut oil to combine. Add the oats, sesame seeds, cinnamon, and salt. Stir the mixture to combine.

4. When it's cool enough to touch, use clean hands to sprinkle the mixture all over the fruit in uneven pieces, covering it completely. Bake until the fruit is bubbling and the crisp is golden brown, 35 to 40 minutes. Cool for about 30 minutes and serve warm with whipped cream or ice cream.

   Note • Leftovers can be refrigerated for up to 1 week.

PLANT
This recipe is vegan.

PLANET
Get creative with seasonal produce. Everything else might be sitting in your pantry already.

NUTRITION, per serving

Calories: 498	Carbs: 68 g	Fiber: 9 g
Fat: 23 g	Protein: 10 g	Sugar: 38 g

Country-Fried Cauliflower & Gravy

When you need a down-home dish, this recipe is every bit as satisfying as it sounds. Fried in a perfectly seasoned batter and smothered in a rich mushroom gravy, cauliflower has never tasted so good. (Plus the joy of saving a chicken!) Just remember: strain your frying oil into a jar to reuse another time or pour it into a disposable container and throw it out. Never pour oil down the drain.

1 large head cauliflower

5 teaspoons kosher salt, plus more to taste

6 tablespoons unsalted butter of choice

1 medium shallot, finely chopped

1 garlic clove, minced

8 ounces baby bella (cremini) mushrooms, caps and stems finely chopped

1 tablespoon finely chopped fresh sage

3 sprigs fresh thyme, leaves picked

2 cups plus 3 tablespoons all-purpose flour

2½ cups milk of choice

Freshly ground black pepper

Vegetable oil, for deep-frying (about 2 quarts)

½ cup cornstarch

2 teaspoons garlic powder (see Powders, page 225)

2 teaspoons onion powder (see Powders, page 225)

2 teaspoons smoked paprika

3 large eggs, beaten

Finely chopped fresh parsley leaves, for serving

1. Remove the outer leaves from the cauliflower and trim the stem so the cauliflower can sit upright on a cutting board. Using a serrated knife, carefully cut the cauliflower in half, then cut each half into 1-inch-thick slabs to create 3 or 4 steaks. Reserve any florets that fall off while cutting.

2. In a Dutch oven, bring 6 cups water to a gentle boil over medium heat. Add 2 teaspoons of the salt. Working in two batches, use tongs to lower the cauliflower steaks into the water. Boil until the stems can be easily pierced with a fork but are still firm, 4 to 5 minutes. Transfer the steaks to paper towels to drain while repeating with the remaining steaks. Finally, boil the reserved florets for 2 to 3 minutes, until tender.

3. Drain the cooking water from the Dutch oven and wipe dry. Set the Dutch oven over medium heat and melt the butter. Add the shallot and garlic and cook, stirring occasionally, until the shallot is softened and the garlic is fragrant, about 2 minutes. Add the mushrooms, sage, thyme, and 1 teaspoon of the salt. Cook, stirring occasionally, until the mushrooms release their juices and brown, about 5 minutes.

4. Add 3 tablespoons of the flour, stirring to coat the mushrooms. Cook until the flour browns and smells nutty, 2 to 3 minutes. Add 2 cups of the milk and stir well to incorporate. Bring to a gentle boil, then reduce the heat to low and simmer until the sauce thickens, about 5 minutes. Season with salt and pepper to taste. Transfer the gravy to a medium bowl and cover to keep warm. Set aside.

5. Wash and dry the Dutch oven. Pour 2 inches of vegetable oil into the Dutch oven and heat over medium-high heat to 375°F.

6. Meanwhile, in a wide shallow bowl, whisk together the remaining 2 cups flour, the cornstarch, garlic powder, onion powder, smoked paprika, and remaining 2 teaspoons salt. In a separate wide shallow bowl, whisk together the eggs and the remaining ½ cup milk.

7. Designate one dry hand and one wet hand. Use the dry hand to set a cauliflower steak in the flour mixture, turning to coat completely. Use the wet hand to dip the steak in the egg mixture, letting any excess egg drip off, before returning to the flour mixture. Use the dry hand once more to dredge thoroughly, shaking off any excess flour or clumps.

8. When the frying oil in the Dutch oven is at temperature, use tongs to lower the steak into the oil. Fry for 3 to 4 minutes before flipping and frying for 2 to 3 more minutes, until both sides are golden brown. Transfer to paper towels to drain. Continue dredging and frying the remaining steaks and florets.

9. Transfer the steaks to serving plates and spoon the gravy over the top. Finish with plenty of black pepper and parsley. Serve the florets with a bowl of the remaining gravy for dunking.

Note • Leftovers can be refrigerated for up to 3 days.

PLANT
This recipe is vegetarian.

PLANET
Cauliflower is at its peak in the fall months. Shop wisely for the other ingredients.

NUTRITION, per serving

| Calories: 1,139 | Carbs: 87 g | Fiber: 8 g |
| Fat: 80 g | Protein: 23 g | Sugar: 7 g |

Strawberry-Rhubarb Blondies

Serves 9

Beautiful *and* delicious, these will quickly become your showstopper dessert of choice. Almost as easy as boxed cake, but with better flavor and less waste, no one needs to know how incredibly simple they are. A strawberry-rhubarb jam practically makes itself on the stove, then gets folded into and swirled on top of a simple blondie batter. There's no better way to welcome spring!

Coconut oil or nonstick cooking spray

Jam

½ pound rhubarb, thinly sliced

½ pound strawberries, thinly sliced

½ cup packed light brown sugar

¼ teaspoon kosher salt

Blondies

1 cup packed light brown sugar

1 large egg

1 teaspoon vanilla extract

½ teaspoon kosher salt

1 stick (4 ounces) unsalted butter, melted

1¼ cups all-purpose flour

¾ cup sliced almonds

½ teaspoon baking powder

1. Set a rack in the center of the oven and preheat to 350°F. Coat an 8 × 8-inch pan with coconut oil or cooking spray.

2. **Make the jam:** In a medium saucepan, combine the rhubarb, strawberries, brown sugar, and salt. Set over medium heat and stir with a wooden spoon to help the sugar melt. The mixture will seem too dry at first, but the heat will quickly liquefy the sugar. Continue to cook, stirring often and using the spoon to mash the fruit, until a thick, jammy mixture forms with a little liquid, about 30 minutes. Transfer to a medium bowl and set aside to cool.

3. **Make the blondies:** In a medium bowl, whisk together the brown sugar, egg, vanilla, and salt. Continue to whisk while pouring in the melted butter. Fold in the flour, ½ cup of the almonds, and the baking powder until just combined. Add ½ cup of the jam and fold 2 or 3 times to swirl it into the batter.

4. Transfer the batter to the prepared pan. Sprinkle the remaining ¼ cup almonds on top. Spoon and gently spread ¼ cup of the jam randomly across the batter for a swirl effect. Bake until the blondies are golden and set, 20 to 25 minutes. Spoon the remaining ¼ cup jam in places over the top. Cool for 10 minutes in the pan, then slice into 9 pieces and serve immediately.

Note • Leftovers can be refrigerated for up to 5 days.

PLANT
This recipe is vegetarian.

PLANET
Strawberries and rhubarb are in season together in the spring. Everything else might be sitting in your pantry already.

NUTRITION, per serving

Calories: 282	Carbs: 49 g	Fiber: 3 g
Fat: 8 g	Protein: 5 g	Sugar: 32 g

Potato Donuts with Fruit Glaze & Basil Sugar

There's no way around it, making donuts is a process. It's a hot, sticky, oily process. But a warm donut out of the fryer? Name a more iconic first bite. Potato donuts, for those who don't know, are amazingly cakey but somehow still so light. Covered in a vibrant fruit glaze and a sprinkle of green basil sugar, these are a work of art that justifies the process. You'll never miss dunking a donut from the store.

Basil sugar

½ cup granulated sugar

¼ cup fresh basil leaves

Glaze

½ pint blackberries

3 cups powdered sugar, plus more as needed

Donuts

2 medium russet potatoes (about 1 pound)

4 tablespoons (½ stick) unsalted butter, at room temperature

¾ cup granulated sugar

1 large egg

2 teaspoons vanilla extract

¼ cup milk of choice

1 tablespoon fresh lemon juice

2½ cups all-purpose flour, plus more for rolling out the dough

1 teaspoon kosher salt

1 teaspoon baking powder

1 teaspoon baking soda

1 teaspoon ground cinnamon

½ teaspoon ground nutmeg

Vegetable oil, for deep-frying (about 2 quarts)

Chopped pistachios, for garnish

1. **Make the basil sugar:** In a food processor, combine the granulated sugar and basil and pulse 4 or 5 times until the basil is in small pieces. Transfer the sugar to a jar and set aside.

2. **Make the glaze:** Rinse the food processor. Add the blackberries and process until fully broken down. Pour the mixture through a fine-mesh sieve into a wide shallow bowl. Use a spatula to press the juices through the sieve, leaving the pulp and seeds behind.

3. Add 2 cups of the powdered sugar and whisk to incorporate. Add more of the powdered sugar 1 tablespoon at a time to achieve a thick glaze that runs in a heavy stream from the whisk. Set aside.

4. **Make the donuts:** Pierce the potatoes all over with a fork. Place the potatoes on a microwave-safe plate and microwave on high for 5 minutes. Use tongs to flip the potatoes and microwave for 5 minutes more until a knife easily slides all the way through. Cut the potatoes in half lengthwise and set aside.

5. In a large bowl, with an electric mixer, cream the butter and granulated sugar until the sugar is dissolved and the butter is fluffy. Add the egg and vanilla and continue mixing until the batter is pale yellow.

-recipe continues-

6. Use a fork to mash the cooked potato. Scoop and lightly pack 1 cup's worth. (Cool and refrigerate the remaining potato for another use.) Add the potato, milk, and lemon juice to the bowl and mix once more to incorporate. Add the flour, salt, baking powder, baking soda, cinnamon, and nutmeg and fold to combine into a cohesive, very sticky dough.

7. Pour 2 inches of oil into a Dutch oven and heat over medium-high heat to 375°F. Set a wire rack over a sheet pan and position near the Dutch oven.

8. Heavily flour a work surface, then turn the dough out. Flour the top of the dough and press into a 14 × 10-inch rectangle. Use a 3-inch biscuit cutter or large drinking glass to cut about 10 rounds from the dough. Use a small cutter or a bottle cap to cut 1-inch donut holes in the centers of the donuts. (Dip the cutters in a bowl of flour before each cut for an easier process.) Peel away the scraps and set them aside.

9. When the oil is at temperature, remove all the donut holes and fry in one batch for about 1 minute, using a spider to flip them every few seconds for even browning. Remove the holes to the wire rack. Working in batches, use a large spatula to slide under 2 donuts, careful not to disturb their shape, and slide them into the oil. Use a spider to flip them every few seconds for even browning. Remove the donuts to the wire rack and repeat with the remaining batches.

10. Reduce the temperature to hold the oil at frying temperature. Press the scraps into a ball, then use wet fingers to press it into an 8 × 6-inch rectangle. Cut 4 donuts and holes. Pull off the scraps and set aside. Bring the oil temperature back to 375°F. Fry the holes, then the donuts in pairs. Ball and press the scraps one more time into a 6 × 4-inch rectangle and cut 2 more donuts and holes. Repeat the frying process once more.

11. When the donuts are cool enough to handle, pour some of the basil sugar into a small bowl and whisk the blackberry glaze to revive it. Working one at a time, dip a donut into the glaze. Let some of the excess drip away, then place the donut back on the wire rack. Sprinkle a pinch of basil sugar over the glaze while it is still wet. Finish with a sprinkling of pistachios. Repeat with the remaining donuts, refilling the sugar bowl as needed. Roll the holes in the glaze and toss in the sugar. (Reserve any remaining sugar for another use.)

Note • Leftovers can be refrigerated for up to 2 days.

PLANT
This recipe is vegetarian.

PLANET
Blackberries are at their best in the summer months, but swap out seasonal berries during the other months.

NUTRITION, per 1 donut + 1 hole

| Calores: 409 | Carbs: 59 g | Fiber: 2 g |
| Fat: 18 g | Protein: 4 g | Sugar: 36 g |

Frozen Cookie Dough

Favorite ice cream flavor? Favorite spatula lick? Favorite I-ate-it-out-of-the-bowl? All of the above? Let's face it, cookie dough is irresistible. This cookie faux is so simple to throw together (you literally throw it together), whip up (in a food processor), and freeze (in bite-size portions), but it's free of the flour, butter, and eggs that make traditional cookie dough such a *guilty* pleasure. These will hit the sweet spot every time.

1 (13.5-ounce) can full-fat coconut milk, well shaken

1½ cups old-fashioned rolled oats

1 cup raw cashews

6 Medjool dates, pitted

¼ cup packed light brown sugar

2 teaspoons vanilla extract

1 teaspoon kosher salt

½ teaspoon ground cinnamon

1 cup semisweet, bittersweet, or dark chocolate chips

1. In a large food storage container, combine the coconut milk, oats, cashews, dates, brown sugar, vanilla, salt, and cinnamon. Stir to combine, cover with an airtight lid, and soak for 8 hours (or up to 24 hours) in the refrigerator.

2. Transfer the mixture to a food processor. Process until a chunky dough forms, about 2 minutes, scraping down the sides as needed. Return to the storage container and fold in the chocolate chips. Return to the refrigerator for about 15 minutes, until the dough is firm.

3. Line a sheet pan with a silicone baking mat or parchment paper. Use a 1-ounce cookie scoop to form 30 equal dough balls on the sheet. Freeze for 2 hours, then transfer to a storage container, separating the layers with parchment paper. Store the dough balls in the freezer for up to 3 months. Enjoy straight out of the freezer as a sweet treat.

PLANT
This recipe is vegan.

PLANET
Everything in this recipe can be sustainably purchased year-round or might be sitting in your pantry already.

NUTRITION, per 2 dough balls

Calories: 233	Carbs: 17 g	Fiber: 1 g
Fat: 13 g	Protein: 3 g	Sugar: 13 g

Whole Roasted Butternut Squash

A stunning presentation, an addictively tangy sauce, an easy side dish. What more could you want? Any seasonal feast, from dinner party to holiday gathering, deserves to have this on the table. Whip up the sauce while the squash roasts, and from there it's just a few flicks of the wrist to a camera-ready dish. It couldn't be easier.

1 medium butternut squash (about 3 pounds)

4 tablespoons olive oil

Kosher salt and freshly ground black pepper

1 medium shallot, finely chopped

3 tablespoons maple syrup

2 tablespoons Dijon mustard

2 tablespoons apple cider vinegar

¼ cup hazelnuts, toasted and roughly chopped

⅓ cup pomegranate seeds

10 fresh chives, thinly sliced

1. Set a rack in the upper third of the oven and preheat to 425°F.

2. Use a vegetable peeler to remove the skin and layer of white flesh (just under the skin) from the butternut squash until the deep-orange flesh is exposed. Cutting through the stem, halve the squash lengthwise. Use a soup spoon to scrape out the seeds and pulp.

3. Place the squash cut-side down on a sheet pan and pour ¼ cup water into the pan. Bake the squash until the flesh is softened but not fully cooked, about 20 minutes.

4. Cool the squash for about 30 minutes, until it can be safely handled. Place one squash half cut-side down on a cutting board. Use a sharp knife to carefully cut thin slits along the squash, about ⅛ inch apart and about halfway through the squash, being careful not to cut all the way through. Repeat with the second half.

5. Brush the baking sheet with 1 tablespoon of the olive oil and return the squash to the pan, cut-side down. Brush 1 more tablespoon of the olive oil all over the squash. Season with salt and pepper. Bake until the squash is fork-tender and golden brown on top, about 35 minutes more.

-recipe continues-

6. While the squash is baking, in a small saucepan, heat the remaining 2 tablespoons olive oil over medium heat until shimmering. Add the shallot, sprinkle with salt, and cook, stirring occasionally, until it begins to brown, 10 to 12 minutes. Add the maple syrup, mustard, and vinegar and whisk to combine. Simmer for about 3 minutes to slightly reduce and thicken the sauce. Season with salt and pepper to taste. Remove from the heat and set aside.

7. When the squash is done, drizzle the warm sauce over the top, making sure to get in between the slits. Finish with the hazelnuts, pomegranate seeds, and chives. Serve immediately, allowing everyone to cut their own portion of squash.

Note • Leftovers can be refrigerated for up to 3 days.

PLANT
This recipe is vegan.

PLANET
Squash is available year-round, but this is a recipe for cold weather.

NUTRITION, per serving

| Calories: 186 | Carbs: 26 g | Fiber: 7 g |
| Fat: 10 g | Protein: 3 g | Sugar: 10 g |

Loaded Breakfast Nachos

Breakfast nachos are ideal at-home brunch fare. They're messy, they're fun, they encourage interaction. It's the perfect dish to loosen up and let the gossip flow. If you know this particular brunch is going to be following a long night, get prepped the day before. The salsa will only improve while marinating in the fridge, and the tofu can be made ahead and reheated. Soak the cashew mixture in the fridge overnight and then blend it up while the chips bake. Done! Work smarter, not hungover.

Cheese

¾ cup raw cashews

½ cup boiling water

¼ cup nutritional yeast

1 tablespoon olive oil

¼ teaspoon kosher salt

Salsa

1 pint cherry or grape tomatoes, quartered

½ medium red onion, finely chopped

4 sprigs fresh cilantro, both stems and leaves, finely chopped

1 jalapeño, seeded and finely chopped

Juice of 1 lime

½ teaspoon kosher salt

Tofu

1 tablespoon olive oil

1 small shallot, finely chopped

1 garlic clove, minced

1 (14-ounce) package extra-firm tofu, drained

1½ teaspoons kosher salt

1 teaspoon ground cumin

1 teaspoon ground turmeric

Nachos

1 (12-ounce) bag tortilla chips

1 (15.5-ounce) can black beans, drained and rinsed, or 1½ cups cooked black beans (see Beans for Days, page 66)

1 avocado, sliced

1. **Make the cheese:** In a blender, combine the cashews, boiling water, nutritional yeast, oil, and salt. Let soak in the blender jar for 30 minutes.

2. **Meanwhile, make the salsa:** In a medium bowl, toss together the tomatoes, onion, cilantro, jalapeño, lime juice, and salt. Set aside to marinate.

3. Set a rack in the center of the oven and preheat to 400°F.

-recipe continues-

4. **Prepare the tofu:** In a medium skillet, heat the oil over medium heat until shimmering. Add the shallot and garlic and cook, stirring occasionally, until the shallot is becoming translucent, about 5 minutes.

5. Crumble the tofu in large clumps into the skillet. Add the salt, cumin, turmeric, and 3 tablespoons water. Stir to combine and cook, stirring occasionally, until the tofu is warmed through and resembles scrambled eggs, about 5 minutes. Remove from the heat and set aside.

6. **Make the nachos:** Arrange the chips on a sheet pan and scatter the black beans on top. Bake until the chips are slightly toasted and the beans are slightly dried and cracked, about 10 minutes.

7. While the chips are baking, blend the cheese on high until a smooth sauce forms, about 1 minute, scraping down the sides as needed.

8. Remove the chips from the oven and spoon the tofu on top. Spoon the salsa on top, leaving as much liquid behind in the bowl as possible. Toss the avocado slices in the reserved salsa liquid, then arrange them on top of the salsa. Drizzle the cheese sauce over everything and serve immediately.

Note • Leftovers can be refrigerated for up to 2 days.

PLANT
This recipe is vegan.

PLANET
For a life-changing and planet-saving salsa, catch cherry tomatoes in the summer months at peak freshness.

NUTRITION, per serving

| Calories: 370 | Carbs: 29 g | Fiber: 11 g |
| Fat: 23 g | Protein: 19 g | Sugar: 3 g |

Broccoli Mac & Cheese

Serves 6 to 8

Broccoli and pasta are a core childhood comfort without rival. And with a vegan cheese sauce made from veggies, there's some deeper nourishment happening here, too. (A boxed mac with powdered cheese is definitely delicious, but also . . . suspicious.) Rich and satisfying, creamy and nurturing, this dish practically begs you to live a little.

⅓ cup bread crumbs or stale bread pulsed in the food processor to make crumbs

2 tablespoons olive oil

1 medium white onion, finely chopped

2 garlic cloves, minced

1 tablespoon plus 2 teaspoons kosher salt, plus more for seasoning

1 medium russet potato, peeled and cut into ½-inch cubes

1 medium carrot, cut into ¼-inch-thick coins

1 cup raw cashews

5 tablespoons nutritional yeast

1 tablespoon white miso

1 tablespoon Dijon mustard

16 ounces elbow macaroni

1 large head broccoli, tough outer layer of the stem peeled, cut into bite-size florets and pieces

Freshly ground black pepper

1. Set a rack in the center of the oven and preheat to 450°F.

2. In a dry 12-inch cast-iron skillet, toast the bread crumbs over medium heat for about 2 minutes, stirring often, as the skillet heats. Transfer to a small bowl and wipe out the skillet.

3. In the same skillet, heat the oil over medium heat until shimmering. Add the onion and garlic, season with 1 teaspoon of the salt, and cook, stirring occasionally, until the onion is translucent and the garlic is fragrant, about 10 minutes.

4. Add the potato, carrot, cashews, and 2 cups water to the skillet. Increase the heat to high and bring to a boil. Reduce the heat to medium and simmer until the potatoes and carrots are very soft and the cashews are swollen, 10 to 15 minutes. Remove from the heat and cool for 10 minutes.

5. Carefully pour the vegetables and liquid into a blender. Add the nutritional yeast, miso, mustard, and 1 teaspoon of the salt. Blend on high for 1 to 2 minutes, until the cheese is smooth and fully incorporated. Set aside.

6. In a large pot, bring 3 quarts water to a boil over high heat. Add the pasta and remaining 1 tablespoon salt. When the pasta is 2 minutes less than al dente according to the package directions, add the broccoli and cook for the remaining 2 minutes.

7. Drain the pasta and broccoli and return to the pot. Pour in the cheese sauce and stir to fully incorporate. Transfer the mac and cheese to the same cast-iron skillet and smooth into an even layer.

8. Use clean hands to toss the toasted bread crumbs with a pinch of salt and a few grinds of black pepper. Sprinkle the seasoned crumbs over the mac and cheese.

9. Bake the mac and cheese until the sauce is bubbling, about 10 minutes. Serve immediately.

Note • Leftovers can be refrigerated for up to 1 week or frozen for up to 6 months.

PLANT
This recipe is vegan.

PLANET
Broccoli can be found at the farmers' market in the spring or fall months. Everything else might be sitting in your pantry already.

NUTRITION, per serving, based on 8 servings

| Calories: 221 | Carbs: 23 g | Fiber: 4 g |
| Fat: 12 g | Protein: 8 g | Sugar: 3 g |

Ben Flanner

Farmer & Cofounder of Brooklyn Grange

Plants! They're amazing. All their different sizes, colors, flavors, textures, and nutrients to marvel at, walk through, cook, eat, and nourish our bodies. As a career farmer, I have developed a lot of affection for plants and the bounties that grow in our Earth's soil.

As a child, my mother had a vegetable garden, and I was the type of kid who couldn't stay out of it. I dug up and rerooted raspberry seedlings from my grandma's house, helped trellis the peas, and was first in line to make (and then eat) the pickles. As I moved into my early adulthood and pursued a degree in industrial engineering, and then a career that had me sitting at a desk, that same natural passion stayed alive as a love of cooking.

When the financial crisis hit in 2008, I decided the time was ripe to reconsider a career in an office. A few weekend trips to farms quickly revived my gardening enthusiasm. I began visiting community gardens, tailoring time out of the city around visits to farms, attending conferences, and devouring farming books. I was energized and filled with some of the greatest resolve I'd had in my entire life: to become a vegetable farmer. Farming represented the ability to move my body, nourish people, solve challenging problems, and interact with plants.

In 2010, I cofounded Brooklyn Grange, the world's largest rooftop soil farm, located on three roofs across Brooklyn and Queens. We grow more than 100,000 pounds of organically cultivated produce each year. So time and motion play a critical element in my daily life as we tackle long to-do lists, meet delivery deadlines, and rotate crops. We tend to thousands of the same plant in one sweep, cultivating weeds with our battery-powered tiller, bunching thousands of radishes for our CSA, or quickly thinning a bed of beets with a hoe.

As much as I have a passion for the systematized growing of vegetables on our 5.6 acres of rooftop space, there is also joy to be found in slowing down and enjoying moments in smaller gardens: helping a friend set up a simple irrigation system with a timer on a hose, harvesting a rainbow chard plant for just one meal's worth of sautéing, or pruning and trellising every single sucker off a tomato or cucumber plant to perfection.

If you have space to grow some of your own food, use that space! From small to large, windowsills, fire escapes, balconies, backyards, front yards, community gardens, or roofs—if there's light, it can grow. You don't need much, and whether it's your indoor pot of basil in a sunny south-facing window, the crop of three kale plants in your backyard, or your tomato plant on your balcony (pro tip: don't try to grow a tomato indoors, friends, there is not enough light coming in through windows), you have direct contact with your food.

Even in small spaces, it's amazing what you can grow. Because Brooklyn Grange started on a single roof, one of the first concepts I learned was growing as much as possible in a finite space. We often grow four different crops in the exact same spot during the course of the season. We might plant radishes first thing in spring after the final deep frost, then swap in a cycle of arugula, then a carrot crop for the late summer, and just before fall we sneak in a quick kohlrabi.

So warm up your little plot of earth with some springtime radishes while your zucchini takes root in its starter pot, bursting and ready to get transplanted. Stick a basil plant wherever it will fit. Same for dill, chives, parsley, sage, and chard (they all work in nooks!). Consider your garden— whatever that looks like for you—a space of opportunity and freedom, where even the smallest crops are the start of an abundant harvest. Happy growing!

Let's
Raise a
Glass

Plant-based drinks that taste better than anything in a can, carton, or plastic bottle. Alcohol-optional (but highly recommended).

Any Fruit Shrub

Shrubs were a popular preservative long before refrigerators were a glimmer in anyone's eye. Sugar sweetens the fruit (and preserves it) while vinegar balances the drink (and also preserves it). With endless mix-and-match possibilities for flavors, shrubs will have you seeing your produce in a whole new light.

1 pound prepared fruit in any combination

2 cups sugar of choice

Herbs and spices (see chart, starting on page 194)

2 cups vinegar of choice

Ice, seltzer, gin, tequila, whiskey, beer, or sparkling wine, for serving

1. In a medium bowl, toss and lightly mash the fruit, sugar, herbs, and spices together. Lay a kitchen towel over the bowl and tightly tuck it underneath to secure. Let the fruit sit at room temperature for 48 hours, stirring halfway through. (The sugar will prevent the fruit from spoiling.)

2. Mash the fruit again and then strain the liquid into a 1-quart jar. Add the vinegar. Taste to adjust for sweetness or acidity. Store the jar in the refrigerator for up to 3 months.

3. To serve, fill a tall glass with ice, then mix your shrub with seltzer or a spirit of choice. Shrubs are also an excellent vinegar substitute in salad dressings (see Dressings, page 220).

-recipe continues-

PLANT
This recipe is vegan.

PLANET
Get creative and swap in fresh, seasonal produce.

NUTRITION, per 2 ounces, using blackberries

Calories: 141	Carbs: 24 g	Fiber: 0 g
Fat: 0 g	Protein: 0 g	Sugar: 34 g

Fruit	Sugar	Herbs & Spices	Vinegar
Apples, peeled, cored, and sliced	Brown	Cinnamon stick, whole cloves, ground nutmeg, grated ginger	Apple cider vinegar
Apricots, pitted and sliced	Brown	Star anise	Rice vinegar
Blackberries	White	Fresh basil	Red vinegar
Blood oranges, peeled and separated	Brown	Fresh thyme	Red wine vinegar
Blueberries	White	Fresh mint	White wine vinegar
Cantaloupe, seeded and cut	White	Fresh tarragon	White wine vinegar
Cherries, pitted	Brown	Ground coffee	Red wine vinegar
Clementines, zested, peeled, and separated	Brown	Clementine zest, grated ginger	Apple cider vinegar
Cranberries	Brown	Cinnamon stick, whole cloves	Apple cider vinegar
Currants	White	Fresh thyme	Red wine vinegar
Figs, halved	Brown	Freshly ground black pepper	Red wine vinegar
Grapefruit, peeled and separated	Brown	Fresh mint, grated ginger	Red wine vinegar
Grapes, halved	White	Fresh rosemary	Apple cider vinegar
Guava, sliced	White	Fresh cilantro	White wine vinegar
Honeydew, seeded and cut	White	Splash of orange flower water	White wine vinegar
Kiwis, peeled and sliced	White	Orange zest, fresh basil	Rice vinegar
Lemons, zested and sliced	White	Lemon zest, lavender	White wine vinegar
Limes, zested and sliced	White	Lime zest, fresh cilantro	White wine vinegar

Fruit	Sugar	Herbs & Spices	Vinegar
Mandarins, peeled and separated	Brown	Star anise	Red wine vinegar
Mangoes, peeled and sliced	White	Hot sauce, lime zest	White wine vinegar
Nectarines, peeled and separated	Brown	Vanilla bean	Red wine vinegar
Papaya, seeded and cut	White	Shredded coconut, grated ginger	Rice vinegar
Peaches, pitted and sliced	White	Bay leaves, fresh basil	White wine vinegar
Pears, peeled, cored, and sliced	Brown	Fennel seeds	Apple cider vinegar
Persimmons, stemmed and sliced	Brown	Whole cloves, vanilla bean	Red wine vinegar
Pineapple, cut	Brown	Allspice, vanilla bean	Rice vinegar
Plums, pitted and sliced	White	Crushed cardamom pods	White wine vinegar
Pomegranate, seeded	Brown	Grated ginger	Red wine vinegar
Prickly pears, peeled and sliced	White	Orange zest, fresh cilantro	White wine vinegar
Raspberries	White	Rose hips	White wine vinegar
Rhubarb, sliced	Brown	Crushed cardamom pods, orange zest	Red wine vinegar
Strawberries, sliced	White	Fresh mint	Red wine vinegar
Tangerines, zested, peeled, and separated	White	Tangerine zest, fresh rosemary	Rice vinegar
Tomatoes	White	Cumin seeds, mustard seeds, red pepper flakes, tamari	White wine vinegar
Watermelon, cut	Brown	Lime zest, chili powder	Apple cider vinegar

Fire Cider

Fire cider packs a fiery punch, but wow is it good for you. Based on a formula that the herbalist Rosemary Gladstar created in the 1970s, it's an all-natural health tonic to keep your system in tip-top shape. Start by drinking a small amount in tea or water to acclimate to the pungent flavors and work up to a daily wellness shot. It's especially great in cold season, taken a few times a day, to fight off any oncoming or lingering sickness.

1 (6-ounce) container prepared horseradish or ¾ cup grated horseradish root

1 large white onion, halved, root and stem removed, peeled, and cut into ½-inch slices

1 head garlic, halved horizontally

1 (5-inch) piece unpeeled fresh ginger, cut croswise into ½-inch slices

2 (2-inch) pieces unpeeled turmeric, halved

2 habanero peppers, stemmed and halved

1 large unpeeled orange, cut into ½-inch slices

1 unpeeled lemon, cut into ½-inch slices

5 sprigs fresh parsley

5 sprigs fresh rosemary

5 sprigs fresh thyme

1 tablespoon black peppercorns

¼ cup maple syrup or raw honey

3 cups apple cider vinegar

1. Place the horseradish in the bottom of a 2-quart jar. Add the onion, garlic, ginger, turmeric, and habaneros. Use the handle of a wooden spoon to gently mash everything down. Add the orange and lemon slices, using the spoon handle to wedge them in around the roots. Add the parsley, rosemary, thyme, peppercorns, and honey. Finally, top it off with the apple cider vinegar, pouring all the way to the brim. Tightly seal the lid and shake the jar.

2. Store the jar in a cool, dark place for 4 weeks. Shake it every day to incorporate the ingredients. When it's ready, set a fine-mesh sieve over a 1-quart jar and pour the liquid into the jar. Discard the contents of the original jar. Store the strained fire cider in the refrigerator for up to 1 year.

Use your Fire Cider as:

- A daily wellness shot
- An addition to tea
- A punchy marinade
- A cocktail mixer
- The acid in salad dressing (see Dressings, page 220)

PLANT
This recipe is vegan.

PLANET
Shop wisely for your produce, make a few batches, and enjoy year-round.

NUTRITION, per 2 ounces

| Calories: 55 | Carbs: 11 g | Fiber: 1 g |
| Fat: 0 g | Protein: 1 g | Sugar: 8 g |

Cranberry Mojito

Makes 1 drink

Nothing feels more festive in cold weather than a sparkling red mojito. Cranberries hit their peak in the fall months, but frozen cranberries can be swapped in anytime. (For an alcohol-free swap, just omit the rum and fill up the glass with seltzer.) A glass of this practically begs for low lights and a mingling party, safely inside from the cold.

Cranberry juice

1 cup fresh cranberries, or thawed frozen cranberries

2 tablespoons maple syrup or raw honey

For 1 cocktail

5 fresh cranberries

6 fresh mint leaves

½ ounce maple syrup or raw honey

1 ounce fresh lime juice

2 ounces light rum

Ice, seltzer, and mint sprig, for serving

1. **Make the cranberry juice:** In a food processor, combine the cranberries, honey, and 1 cup water. Process on high until a smooth mixture forms, about 2 minutes. Set a fine-mesh sieve over a large bowl. Set a tea towel in the sieve. Pour the juice into the tea towel, then gather the corners and squeeze the pulp to extract any remaining juice. Store the juice in an airtight container in the refrigerator for up to 2 weeks.

2. **Make a cocktail:** Place the cranberries, mint, and honey in the bottom of a tall glass. Use a muddler or the handle of a wooden spoon to gently burst the cranberries and release the oils from the mint, without breaking the leaves too much. Add the lime juice, rum, and 2 ounces of cranberry juice. Fill the glass halfway with ice and gently stir a few times to combine the ingredients. Fill the glass the rest of the way with ice and top off with seltzer. Garnish with a mint sprig.

PLANT
This recipe is vegan.

PLANET
Cranberries are at their best in the fall months, but frozen cranberries work just as well.

NUTRITION, per serving

| Calories: 245 | Carbs: 29 g | Fiber: 5 g |
| Fat: 1 g | Protein: 3 g | Sugar: 20 g |

Homemade Vegetable Juice

Vegetable juice is great in any form, but the fresher the vegetables, the higher the benefits. Make this juice at the height of summer when the farmers' market is bursting with nutrients. And for an extra treat, remember the immortal words "A spoonful of vodka helps the vegetables go down."

2 large beefsteak tomatoes, cored and quartered

1 medium carrot, cut into 2-inch pieces

1 celery stalk, cut into 2-inch pieces

1 red bell pepper, cut into strips

1 cup baby spinach

Juice of 1 lemon

1 teaspoon kosher salt

Gin, vodka, or beer and hot sauce, for serving (optional)

1. In a high-powered blender, combine the tomatoes and ½ cup water. Blend on high for about 30 seconds until the tomatoes are broken down. Add the carrot, celery, bell pepper, spinach, lemon juice, and salt. Blend on high for 1 to 2 minutes until a smooth mixture forms.

2. Pour the juice and pulp into a large jar. (Alternatively, set a fine-mesh sieve over the jar to strain out the pulp.) Seal tightly and store in the refrigerator for up to 1 week. Shake well before serving, with an optional splash of spirits.

PLANT
This recipe is vegan.

PLANET
Make this in the summer months when produce, especially tomatoes, is at peak freshness.

NUTRITION, per serving

Calories: 69	Carbs: 16 g	Fiber: 1 g
Fat: 1 g	Protein: 3 g	Sugar: 9 g

Verde Marys

More complex and intriguing than a typical bloody, the ingredients slide under the broiler to bring a smoky char into the glass. Cucumber adds refreshment, while vinegar, tamari, and horseradish add savory punches. You'll never be seeing red again!

1 pound tomatillos, husked

1 jalapeño, halved and seeded

1 garlic clove

2 scallions, root ends trimmed

1 medium English cucumber, quartered

¼ cup white wine vinegar

2 tablespoons tamari

2 tablespoons prepared horseradish

1 tablespoon kosher salt

Cocktails

Ice

2 ounces vodka or seltzer per cocktail

Hot sauce

Celery sticks and lime wheels, for serving

1. Preheat the broiler to high.

2. Arrange the tomatillos, jalapeño, garlic, and scallions on a sheet pan. Place under the broiler for about 5 minutes until everything is nicely charred.

3. Add the contents of the sheet pan to a blender along with the cucumber, vinegar, tamari, horseradish, and salt. Blend on high for about 1 minute to form a cohesive liquid. Pour into a pitcher.

4. **Make a cocktail:** Fill tall glasses with ice. Into each one, pour ¾ cup of the tomatillo mixture. Top with the vodka (or seltzer for a nonalcoholic drink) and stir to combine. Garnish each with a splash of hot sauce, a celery stick, and a lime wheel and serve immediately.

Note • The tomatillo mixture can be refrigerated for up to 1 week.

PLANT
This recipe is vegan.

PLANET
Make this in the summer months when produce, especially tomatillos, is at peak freshness.

NUTRITION, per serving, without alcohol

| Calories: 59 | Carbs: 11 g | Fiber: 3 g |
| Fat: 1 g | Protein: 3 g | Sugar: 6 g |

Slice Shots

If you thought you graduated from Jell-O shots when you got your diploma, think again. These vegan shots, nestled in lemon and lime slices, are the cutest little temptation you'll ever see. Lemon-vodka and lime-tequila shots are the perfect backyard treat to make any party extra memorable. (Or unmemorable, depending on how many you take.)

3 large limes, halved lengthwise

3 medium lemons, halved lengthwise

½ cup sugar

2 teaspoons agar-agar powder

½ cup vodka or seltzer

½ cup tequila or seltzer

Kosher salt

1. Run a paring knife around the fruit of the lime and lemon halves, careful not to pierce the rind. Use a spoon to scoop the fruit into separate bowls, leaving a scooped-out rind. Set the rinds aside.

2. Squeeze the juice from the lemon fruit into a small saucepan and discard the pulp (some pulp in the saucepan is fine). Add ¼ cup of the sugar and 1 teaspoon of the agar-agar and set the pan over low heat. Without stirring, let the sugar melt and the agar-agar dissolve, until the mixture just begins to bubble. Pour the mixture back into the lemon bowl. Repeat with the lime fruit and the remaining ¼ cup sugar and 1 teaspoon agar-agar. To the lemon bowl, add the vodka (or seltzer for a virgin shot). To the lime bowl, add the tequila or seltzer.

3. Fill a serving platter with several cups of kosher salt. Press each rind half into the salt to create an even, steady base. Pour the lime mixture into a spouted measuring cup or small pitcher, then fill each lime half with the mixture. Rinse out the measuring cup and repeat with the lemon halves and mixture. Refrigerate for 4 hours or up to 24 hours.

4. When ready to serve, cut each fruit half in half to create wedges. Nestle them into the salt and serve immediately. Use the salt on the tray to sprinkle on your hand, or dip the wedge into the salt before eating it.

Note • Slice shots can be refrigerated in an airtight container for up to 1 week.

PLANT
This recipe is vegan.

PLANET
Lemons and limes are commonly found year-round, and it's always the right time for a Slice Shot.

NUTRITION, Lime Slice Shots with tequila, 1 shot

Calories: 36	Carbs: 5 g	Fiber: 0 g
Fat: 0 g	Protein: 0 g	Sugar: 4 g
		Alcohol: 2 g

NUTRITION, Lemon Slice Shots with vodka, 1 shot

Calories: 40	Carbs: 5 g	Fiber: 0 g
Fat: 0 g	Protein: 0 g	Sugar: 4 g
		Alcohol: 3 g

NUTRITION, Nonalcoholic Slice Shots

| Calories: 19 | Carbs: 5 g | Fiber: 0 g |
| Fat: 0 g | Protein: 0 g | Sugar: 5 g |

Carrot Mimosas

Makes 4 drinks

An orange-carrot blend perks up the familiar mimosa just enough to make things interesting, without getting weird. Plus, in the middle of winter, it's a great multitasking drink: nature's pick-me-up (champagne) plus nature's medicine cabinet (vitamins and minerals).

2 medium oranges, peeled and quartered

2 medium carrots, coarsely chopped

1 (750 ml) bottle sparkling wine or seltzer

1. In a blender, combine the oranges and carrots and blend on high until a smooth mixture forms, about 2 minutes. Pour the juice through a fine-mesh sieve into a pitcher.

2. Divide the juice among four glasses, about ½ cup per glass. Top off with sparkling wine.

Note • The orange-carrot juice can be refrigerated for up to 1 week.

PLANT
This recipe is vegan.

PLANET
Oranges are at their peak in the winter months, right when you need the vitamin boost the most.

NUTRITION, per serving

Calories: 172	Carbs: 13 g	Fiber: 0 g
Fat: 0 g	Protein: 1 g	Sugar: 7 g
		Alcohol: 17 g

Hibiscus-Cherry Electro-ade

Packed with all the super benefits of hibiscus and cherries, plus the electrolytes of coconut water, this is a power drink that is as delicious as it is good for you. A little honey and lime sweeten the deal and a bit of sea salt enhances the electrolyte benefits. Keep a jar in the fridge for a quick boost anytime!

2 tablespoons dried hibiscus flowers or contents of 6 bags hibiscus tea (removed from bags)

⅓ cup pitted cherries, fresh or frozen thawed

1 tablespoon maple syrup or raw honey

¾ cup fresh lime juice (about 6 limes)

1 liter coconut water

½ teaspoon sea salt

1. In a food processor, combine the hibiscus, cherries, honey, and 1 cup water (not coconut water). Let the hibiscus infuse for 10 minutes, until the liquid is deep red. Process on high until a chunky mixture forms, about 2 minutes.

2. Set a fine-mesh sieve over a large bowl. Set a tea towel in the sieve. Pour the juice into the tea towel, then gather the corners and squeeze the pulp to extract any remaining juice.

3. Pour the juice into a large pitcher. Whisk in the lime juice, coconut water, and salt. Serve chilled.

   Note • The electro-ade can be refrigerated for up to 1 week.

PLANT
This recipe is vegan.

PLANET
Cherries are at their best in the summer months, but frozen cherries work just as well.

NUTRITION, per serving

Calories: 83	Carbs: 20 g	Fiber: 0 g
Fat: 1 g	Protein: 2 g	Sugar: 13 g

EXPERT
OPINION
FROM

David Zilber

Chef, Author,
Fermenter &
Food Scientist

You want to judge a chef's worth?
Look in his waste bin.

This old adage is something I've heard thrown around kitchens since I started cooking at a fancy pan-Asian (it was beneath the chef to call it fusion) restaurant in

Toronto in the early aughts. Tales the older chefs would tell about their battle-hardened former mentors: grumpy men who'd cut their teeth in the '80s. But back then, the sentiment wasn't about sustainability (in today's sense of the word) but economy. Restaurants have always been a tough place to hack out a living, and most of these old dogs saw it as nothing more than smart business sense to turn plum skins into plum jam, carrot peelings into carrot chips, or pigskin into crackling.

Today, the sensibility of knowing that every gram of every food to come through your door has value gets diminished in part by food's low cost. It doesn't *feel* like the few leftovers of less-than-freshest strawberries in the carton would cost you much to toss, because they cost so little to begin with; but the costs lie elsewhere, external to your supermarket, your fridge, and your daily life. We're just now learning that the bill is coming due in other ways. Instead of reducing waste out of fiscal responsibility, we have an obligation to reduce it out of collective responsibility.

Back in your great-grandmum's days, when "organic food" was just "food," the average American spent about 30 percent of their income to feed themselves. Today, that number is under 10 percent! That missing 20-something percent *is* being paid, but not by us . . . yet. We are overdrawing our accounts from the soil, air, and ecosystem and will keep going until they're bankrupt. When that happens, it will already be too late.

But it's not all doom and gloom! The easiest way to go about enacting *real, lasting, habitual change* is to start thinking about your food like it *did* cost three times as much. If you imagine that part of your budget through that lens, you'll start to train yourself to think creatively about every gram of food to pass through your hands—not as a curmudgeonly caricature of a tired old chef, but as someone educated enough to take personal responsibility for the mark they leave on the world.

It's that creative spark, born of seeing something as simple as a broccoli stalk for the true value of what it took to grow it, that will make a sustainable lifestyle feel not like a chore, but a pleasure. Dare yourself to use every piece of every whole food you put into your fridge! Save up scraps in your freezer until you have enough to make a soup! Or a kraut! There are so many avenues available to us already, right at (and on!) our fingertips to help us reduce our waste in kitchens, it just takes a bit of waking up to. That was the shift in perception I experienced for myself as a chef, when I started working with fermentation at Noma in Copenhagen. Running the Fermentation Lab there taught me to look at the second life of everything around me. Using the very microbes in my surroundings to coax out the delicious acids that would keep Noma's foods lasting longer. Finding ways to extend the life of all we could, to hold on to its value like savings in a bank.

Salting, pickling, and fermenting are just some of the tools all of us have at our disposal; tools that cost us so little, and gain us so much. I implore everyone to work just that little bit to see the pleasure in reducing waste through preservation, and see it as a democratic and creative art we all get to add our flair to.

The Preservation Society

Everything you need to know
to make your produce last.

Pickles

Pickles are so useful to have on hand. They lift up a cheese plate, elevate a salad, perk up a sandwich, dress up a dip, or just make snack time more fun. With a simple base brine and endless flavor pairings, stray produce will be hanging out in the pickle jar within minutes and rewarding you for months.

1 cup cold water

1 cup distilled white vinegar

1 tablespoon kosher salt

1 tablespoon sugar

Produce (see Pairing Ideas on page 214)

Herbs and spices (see Pairing Ideas on page 214)

1. In a medium saucepan, combine the water, vinegar, salt, and sugar and bring to a boil over high heat.

2. Meanwhile, chop the vegetables. Add the vegetables to a 1-pint screw-top jar, packing everything in tightly, then add the spices.

3. Ladle the boiling brine into the jar, filling it to the brim. Tightly screw on the lid and turn the jar upside down to cool. After about 1 hour, turn right-side up and transfer to the refrigerator. The pickles will be ready to eat in 1 week and can be stored in the refrigerator for up to 3 months.

Note • Use a clean jar! Either run it through the dishwasher or boil in a large pot of water for 15 minutes.

-recipe continues-

PLANT
This recipe is vegan.

PLANET
Shop wisely and pickle in-season produce for the fall and winter months.

NUTRITION, per 2 cups, using cucumber

| Calories: 31 | Carbs: 5 g | Fiber: 0 g |
| Fat: 0 g | Protein: 0 g | Sugar: 4 g |

Pairing Ideas

Beets	+	mustard seeds	+	fennel fronds	+ coriander seeds
Bell peppers	+	coriander seeds	+	mustard seeds	+ red pepper flakes
Carrot	+	mustard seeds	+	cinnamon stick	+ coriander seeds
Cauli-flower	+	black pepper-corns	+	ground turmeric	+ coriander seeds
Cucumber	+	black pepper-corns	+	fresh dill	+ smashed garlic cloves
Fennel	+	black pepper-corns	+	orange peel	+ coriander seeds
Grapes	+	black pepper-corns	+	fresh rosemary	+ coriander seeds
Green beans	+	black pepper-corns	+	fresh dill	+ red pepper flakes
Jalapeños	+	black pepper-corns	+	mustard seeds	+ smashed garlic cloves
Okra	+	black pepper-corns	+	mustard seeds	+ coriander seeds
Radishes	+	mustard seeds	+	fresh mint	+ coriander seeds
Red onions	+	black pepper-corns	+	smashed garlic cloves	+ fresh thyme

Kraut

Kraut, like its cooler cousin kimchi, is a miracle of gut health. They're both cabbage-based and are created by the same bacterial process, called lacto-fermentation—and thus offer the same health benefits for a happy gut. And similar to Spicy Braised Cabbage (page 156), a batch of kraut answers the age-old question: What do I do with the rest of this cabbage?

1 medium head cabbage (about 3 pounds)

1½ tablespoons kosher salt

Vegetables and spices (see Pairing Ideas)

1. Remove two of the large outer leaves of the cabbage and set aside. Cut the cabbage into quarters and trim out the core. Thinly slice the cabbage into ribbons.

2. In a medium bowl, combine the cabbage, salt, and any additional vegetables and spices. Toss to distribute the salt, then cover the bowl with a kitchen towel and let rest for 30 minutes, until the cabbage has softened.

3. Remove the towel and massage the cabbage to release as much liquid as possible. Cover and let rest for another 30 minutes, then massage once more.

4. Divide the cabbage evenly between two 1-quart jars, then pour the liquid evenly over the cabbage. Take the reserved cabbage leaves and press one inside each jar to keep the cabbage submerged below the liquid, making sure the leaf covers the entire surface area of the jar. Lightly screw on the lid, but leave it loose to allow gas to escape.

5. Store the jars in a cool, dark place for 4 to 6 days, or until it tastes perfect, checking to make sure the cabbage is always submerged. The kraut might bubble, foam, or form a thin white scum on top. This is all normal and can be skimmed away before refrigerating. If any fuzzy mold forms, play it safe and start over. As long as the cabbage stays submerged, there should not be any mold. Transfer to the refrigerator and store for up to 3 months.

Note • Use clean jars! Either run them through the dishwasher or boil them in a large pot of water for 15 minutes.

Pairing Ideas

Green cabbage	+	caraway seeds	+	grated turmeric
Red cabbage	+	grated beet	+	grated garlic
Green cabbage	+	grated carrot	+	grated ginger
Red cabbage	+	fennel seeds	+	grated apple

PLANT
This recipe is vegan.

PLANET
Make this a zero-waste recipe by shopping package-free.

NUTRITION, per serving

Calories: 39	Carbs: 9 g	Fiber: 3 g
Fat: 0 g	Protein: 2 g	Sugar: 5 g

Nut Butters

We're all familiar with the classic almond butter. But did you know pecans, pistachios, and walnuts all make delicious butters, too? A nut butter made simply with toasted nuts and a little salt is already perfect, but finding the right mix of herbs and spices can take it to sublime heights. Some of our favorite pairings are listed below.

4 cups raw nuts, such as almonds, cashews, hazelnuts, peanuts, pecans, pistachios, or walnuts

1 teaspoon kosher salt

Additional flavorings (see Pairing Ideas)

1. Set a rack in the center of the oven and preheat to 350°F.

2. Spread the nuts over a sheet pan. Bake until the nuts are slightly toasted and fragrant, about 5 minutes, stirring the nuts and rotating the pan front to back halfway through. Transfer the nuts to a blender or food processor and add the salt.

3. If using a blender, start at the lowest speed to form a crumbly mixture, about 1 minute. Blend for 4 to 5 minutes more, gradually increasing the speed to high and stopping to scrape down the sides as needed, until a smooth mixture forms.

4. If using a food processor, process until a coarse meal forms, about 2 minutes. Let the food processor cool for 5 minutes to avoid machine burnout. Then process until the nuts go from a coarse mixture to a loose ball to a smooth paste, 8 to 10 minutes more, stopping to scrape down the sides as needed.

5. Add any additional flavorings and blend or process for about 1 minute to incorporate. Transfer the nut butter to a jar, tighten the lid, and refrigerate for up to 2 weeks.

Note • Use clean jars! Either run them through the dishwasher or boil them in a large pot of water for 15 minutes.

Pairing Ideas

Almonds	+	grated ginger	+	ground cardamom
Cashews	+	shredded coconut	+	curry powder
Hazelnuts	+	melted chocolate	+	brown sugar
Peanuts	+	honey	+	cinnamon
Pecans	+	maple syrup	+	rosemary
Pistachios	+	cardamom	+	vanilla
Walnuts	+	orange zest	+	thyme

PLANT
This recipe is vegan.

PLANET
Everything in this recipe can be sustainably purchased year-round or might be sitting in your pantry already.

NUTRITION, per tablespoon, using almonds

Calories: 79	Carbs: 3 g	Fiber: 2 g
Fat: 7 g	Protein: 3 g	Sugar: 1 g

Jams

Making jam is as easy as boiling fruit and sugar. That's it. No pectin, no water-sealing jars. Of course by simplifying the process, this means your jam has to live in the refrigerator instead of on the pantry shelf. But in every other way, you'll have a real-deal jam ready to spread on toast or swirl in yogurt. Go ahead, load up on an extra pound or two of fruit at the farmers' market!

1 pound fruit, any combination, such as berries (blackberries, blueberries, raspberries, or sliced strawberries) or stone fruit (pitted and halved cherries, or peeled, pitted, and chopped apricots, nectarines, peaches, or plums)

½ cup sugar of choice

Herbs, spices, and flavorings (see Pairing Ideas)

1. Place a small dish in the freezer.

2. In a medium saucepan, combine the fruit and sugar. Use a potato masher to gently crush the fruit and release the juices. Let rest at room temperature for 10 minutes to macerate.

3. Set the saucepan over medium heat and bring to a boil, stirring often. Continue to boil, stirring often, until the mixture is thick, 25 to 30 minutes. Remove the dish from the freezer and spoon a small pool of jam on it. Wait a few seconds, then run the spoon through the jam. If the trail stays separated, the jam is ready. If the trail pools back together, continue to boil and stir a few more minutes.

4. Add any herbs, spices, or flavorings to an empty 1-pint jar. Immediately transfer the jam to the jar and set the lid on top, but don't seal it. Let cool for 1 hour before sealing and transferring to the refrigerator. The jam can be stored in the refrigerator for up to 1 month. (Alternatively, transfer the cooked jam to a straight-sided jar, with no shoulders, leaving about 1 inch of space at the top. Cool, then freeze the jam for up to 6 months. Place the jam in the refrigerator for 24 hours to thaw, then consume within 1 month. Do not refreeze the jam after thawing.)

Note • Use a clean jar! Either run it through the dishwasher or boil in a large pot of water for 15 minutes.

Pairing Ideas

Apricots	+	split vanilla bean	+	cinnamon stick
Blackberries	+	basil	+	bourbon
Blueberries	+	lavender	+	lemon peel
Cherries	+	thyme	+	mint
Nectarines	+	cardamom pod	+	sage
Peaches	+	grated ginger	+	rosemary
Plums	+	star anise	+	whole cloves
Raspberries	+	jalapeño	+	mint
Strawberries	+	balsamic vinegar	+	black pepper

PLANT
This recipe is vegan.

PLANET
Shop wisely for your produce and freeze in-season jams for the fall and winter months.

NUTRITION, per ¼ cup, from 1 pound strawberries

Calories: 67	Carbs: 17 g	Fiber: 1 g
Fat: 0 g	Protein: 0 g	Sugar: 15 g

Dressings

Once you get the hang of the dressing formula, the riffing possibilities are endless. As demonstrated in the Pairing Ideas opposite, a dressing base doesn't have to start with oil. Begin by looking at your refrigerator as an endless landscape of potential dressings, and never face a boring salad again!

½ cup **Base** (see chart)

¼ cup **Acid** (see chart)

½ teaspoon **kosher salt**

¼ teaspoon **freshly ground black pepper**

Additional flavorings (see chart)

1. In a screw-top pint jar, combine the base, acid, salt, pepper, and any additional flavorings. Shake vigorously for 30 seconds to mix and emulsify.

2. Taste for seasoning. Use immediately or seal tightly and refrigerate for up to 2 weeks.

PLANT
This recipe can be made fully vegan.

PLANET
Shop wisely for your produce; most things can be sustainably purchased year-round.

Pairing Ideas

Base	Acid	Flavorings	Notes
Avocado	Lemon juice	¼ cup water, 1 garlic clove, ½ teaspoon Dijon mustard, 1 tablespoon each finely chopped fresh chives, parsley, and dill	Blend until smooth
Fresh orange juice	Rice vinegar	1 tablespoon tamari, 1 teaspoon sesame oil	Omit salt
Olive oil	Balsamic vinegar	1 teaspoon dried oregano, 1 teaspoon Dijon mustard	
Olive oil	Fire Cider (page 197)	2 tablespoons maple syrup, 1 teaspoon Dijon mustard	
Olive oil	Lemon juice	1 teaspoon curry powder	
Olive oil	Lemon juice	1 teaspoon dried oregano, 1 grated garlic clove	
Olive oil	Red wine vinegar	1 teaspoon Dijon mustard, 1 grated garlic clove	
Olive oil	White miso	¼ cup rice vinegar, 2 tablespoons tamari, 1 teaspoon grated fresh ginger	Omit salt
Shredded carrots	Rice vinegar	½ cup refined coconut oil, 1 tablespoon grated fresh ginger	Blend until smooth
Soft tofu	Rice vinegar	¼ cup water, 3 tablespoons miso, 2 tablespoons grated fresh ginger	Omit salt, blend until smooth
Tahini	Lemon juice	¼ cup water, 1 tablespoon maple syrup	
Yogurt	Shrub (page 193)	2 tablespoons water, 1 teaspoon Dijon mustard	

Hot Sauces

In its most basic form, a hot sauce is chile peppers, vinegar, garlic, sweetener, and salt. But where it gets interesting is expanding the produce to contrast or complement the chiles. For milder hot sauce, lean heavily on other produce and include a small amount of chiles. For an atomic hot sauce, go heavy on the chiles and cut them with some produce. (Or don't!) Then start expanding into new vinegars, new sweeteners, flavored salts. The possibilities are endless.

½ pound produce, in any combination (see chart), trimmed of stems and inedible parts (but chile seeds retained) and thinly sliced

½ cup apple cider vinegar

2 garlic cloves, smashed

1 tablespoon kosher salt

1 tablespoon raw honey, maple syrup, or sugar of choice

1. In a medium saucepan, combine the produce, vinegar, garlic, salt, honey, and 2 cups water and bring to a boil over high heat. Reduce the heat to low and simmer until the garlic and produce are soft, about 10 minutes.

2. Pour the mixture into a blender and cool for about 10 minutes, until the steam has settled. Set the lid on the blender, but remove the steam vent from the center and use a folded kitchen towel to cover the hole. Blend until the sauce is smooth.

3. Set a fine-mesh sieve over a measuring cup. Pour the sauce through the sieve, using a spatula to press the liquid through. Discard the solids.

4. Pour the sauce into bottles or jars and set the lid on top but don't seal it. Cool for 1 hour before sealing and transferring to the refrigerator. The hot sauce can be stored in the refrigerator for up to 1 month. (Alternatively, transfer the cooked hot sauce to a straight-sided jar, with no shoulders, leaving about 1 inch of space at the top. Cool, then freeze the hot sauce for up to 6 months. Place the hot sauce in the refrigerator for 24 hours to thaw, then consume within 1 month. Do not refreeze the hot sauce after thawing.)

Note • Use clean jars! Either run them through the dishwasher or boil them in a large pot of water for 15 minutes.

Pairing Ideas

Carrot	+	serrano pepper
Green bell pepper	+	jalapeño pepper
Mango	+	habanero pepper
Peach	+	ají amarillo chile
Pineapple	+	serrano pepper

NUTRITION, per tablespoon, using hot peppers

Calories: 6	Carbs: 1 g	Fiber: 0 g
Fat: 0 g	Protein: 0 g	Sugar: 1 g

PLANT
This recipe can be made fully vegan.

PLANET
Shop wisely for your produce and freeze in-season hot sauces for the off-season.

Dehydrating

The #1 reason to learn to dehydrate is that horrifying moment when your herbs are growing faster than you can use them. (If you don't have an herb garden, or you're feeling sensitive because you just killed them all, ignore that sentence and start with this next one.) Dehydrating is the best way to make fresh flavors stretch long past their normal shelf life. Dried herbs, citrus, garlic, and onions are incredible flavor boosters to have on hand. Dried fruit is snack heaven. And dried mushrooms are especially handy for any impromptu risotto, pasta, or ramen that needs an extra oomph.

Any amount of fresh herbs, citrus peels, sliced fruit, garlic, onions, or mushrooms

1. Set a rack in the center of the oven and preheat to 150°F, or as low as possible.

2. Arrange the items on a baking sheet or pizza stone, leaving plenty of room for air to circulate around the items. Slide the sheet into the oven and close the oven door almost all the way. (If your oven door won't stay open, use the handle of a wooden spoon to prop it open.)

3. After 1 hour, rotate the baking sheet front to back and flip the items over to dehydrate the opposite side. Continue to rotate and flip every hour until the items are dry and crisp. Some herbs will be ready after the first hour; some fruit can take up to 3 hours.

4. Herbs can be removed from their stems, crumbled, and stored in an airtight container for up to 3 months. Citrus peels can be chopped and stored in an airtight container for up to 1 month. Fruit can be stored whole in an airtight container for up to 2 months. Garlic and onion slices can be chopped and stored in airtight containers for up to 3 months. Mushrooms can be stored whole in an airtight container for up to 2 months.

Ideas

Dried rosemary, thyme, and oregano are great for omelets or roasting vegetables.

Dried basil, dill, and parsley are great for dressings or dips.

Dried orange, lemon, and lime are great for marinades or tea.

Dried fruit is great for scones or hot cereal.

Dried garlic and onions are great for stews or grains.

Dried mushrooms are great for risotto or ramen.

PLANT
This recipe is vegan.

PLANET
This is a zero-waste recipe; dehydrate in-season items to enjoy later.

Powders

After dehydrating, making a powder is often a great next step. Powders, like onion powder or garlic powder, are incredible. Mushroom powder is an umami secret weapon you can sneak into anything savory. And then the final transformative step is making a flavored salt. (Lemon salt? Thyme salt? Shiitake salt? Um, yes.) As always, let your instincts and imagination lead you down every path worth exploring!

Any amount of dehydrated herbs, citrus peels, sliced fruit, garlic, onions, or mushrooms (see Dehydrating, opposite)

Kosher salt (optional)

1. The best tools are a spice grinder, a thoroughly cleaned coffee grinder, or a mortar and pestle. A blender will work for larger amounts, but the other methods are still preferable.

2. Add the item to the vessel of choice. If making a flavored salt, add salt in equal proportion to the item. Grind for 30 seconds to 1 minute until a fine powder forms. Set a fine-mesh sieve over a jar and pour the powder through. Tap to shake out all the powder. Transfer any remaining solids to the grinder, grind again, and pass through the sieve. Repeat until everything is a fine powder.

3. Powders can be stored in airtight containers for up to 1 month. Salts can be stored in airtight containers for up to 3 months.

Ideas

Powdered herbs are great for wellness shots.

Powdered citrus is great for smoothies.

Powdered fruit is great for decorating desserts.

Powdered garlic and onions are great for dry rubs.

Powdered mushrooms are great for popcorn.

PLANT
This recipe is vegan.

PLANET
This is a zero-waste recipe; process in-season items to enjoy later.

Bread &
Butter

A perfectly set table isn't
complete without bread
to break and butter to pass.

Cacio e Pepe Socca

A Mediterranean staple, socca is a simply prepared flatbread made from chickpea flour. No kneading, no rising, and a quick bake make it very approachable for any level of baker. Merged with another Mediterranean staple, cacio e pepe—which literally means "cheese and pepper"—this socca soars with savory Parmesan and the bite of black pepper. For an easy vegan swap, skip the cheese and use 2 tablespoons of freshly chopped herbs instead.

1 cup chickpea flour (see Note)

½ cup grated Parmesan cheese

4 tablespoons olive oil

2 teaspoons freshly ground black pepper

1 teaspoon kosher salt

1. Set a rack in the center of the oven and place a 12-inch cast-iron skillet on the rack. Preheat the oven to 450°F.

2. In a medium bowl, add the chickpea flour. Slowly pour in 1 cup water while whisking to prevent lumps. Whisk in ¼ cup of the Parmesan, 2 tablespoons of the olive oil, 1 teaspoon of the black pepper, and the salt. Let the mixture soak for 30 minutes.

3. Carefully remove the skillet from the oven. Add the remaining 2 tablespoons olive oil to the hot skillet and swirl to coat. Pour the batter into the center of the skillet, letting it travel to the edges. Swirl the pan to evenly coat with the batter, then return to the oven. Bake until evenly cooked, about 10 minutes. Turn the oven to broil and broil until nicely browned on the edges, 1 to 2 minutes.

4. Remove from the oven and finish the socca with the remaining ¼ cup Parmesan and 1 teaspoon black pepper. Slice into 6 pieces and serve immediately. Leftovers can be refrigerated for up to 1 week.

Note • Having trouble getting your hands on chickpea flour? Make your own! Process dried chickpeas in a food processor for about 3 minutes, then sift through a fine-mesh sieve to catch any big pieces. Continue to process and sift until you have what you need. For the 1 cup chickpea flour called for here, you'll need about ⅔ cup dried chickpeas.

PLANT
This recipe can be made fully vegan.

PLANET
Making your own chickpea flour saves time, money, and packaging. Win, win, win!

NUTRITION, per slice

| Calories: 176 | Carbs: 10 g | Fiber: 2 g |
| Fat: 12 g | Protein: 6 g | Sugar: 2 g |

Herbed Corn Bread

This simple skillet corn bread bursts with surprises. Corn kernels add wonderful texture while herbs give it a lift of new and exciting flavors. Feel free to play with whatever you have—chives, rosemary, and sage would all be excellent here.

8 tablespoons (1 stick) unsalted butter of choice

2 large eggs

2 tablespoons raw honey or sugar of choice

1 garlic clove, grated

1½ teaspoons kosher salt

1 cup buttermilk or 1 cup milk of choice with 1 tablespoon fresh lemon juice

1 cup white or yellow cornmeal

1 cup all-purpose flour

2 teaspoons baking powder

½ teaspoon baking soda

1 cup corn kernels, frozen or fresh

4 scallions, thinly sliced

1 cup loosely packed fresh basil leaves, finely chopped

½ cup loosely packed fresh dill fronds, finely chopped

10 sprigs fresh thyme, stems removed

1. Set a rack in the center of the oven and preheat to 400°F.

2. In a 12-inch cast iron skillet, melt the butter over low heat. Once the butter is melted, swirl to coat the skillet and remove from the heat.

3. In a large bowl, whisk together the eggs, honey, garlic, and salt until the eggs are well beaten. Add the buttermilk and melted butter and whisk to combine. Add the cornmeal, flour, baking powder, and baking soda and whisk until just incorporated. Use a spatula to fold in the corn, scallions, basil, dill, and thyme.

4. Scrape the batter into the prepared skillet and transfer to the oven. Bake until a toothpick inserted into the center comes out clean, 25 to 30 minutes.

5. Cool for 20 minutes in the skillet before cutting into 8 slices and serving warm.

Note • Leftovers can be refrigerated for up to 1 week.

PLANT
This recipe is vegetarian.

PLANET
Fresh corn can be used in the summer months and frozen corn works great year-round. Freeze your own in the summer months for year-round sustainability.

NUTRITION, per serving

| Calories: 293 | Carbs: 37 g | Fiber: 3 g |
| Fat: 14 g | Protein: 7 g | Sugars: 7 g |

Spinach & Artichoke Rolls

For the dairy-free among us, these rolls provide all the warm, gooey goodness of a spinach and artichoke dip wrapped in a soft whole wheat roll. (And if dairy is your thing, skip the cashew cheese and use an 8-ounce package of organic cream cheese instead.) The recipe makes 9 rolls, which means plenty to last you all week when the carb cravings strike. Or you could share them, but only if you want.

Rolls

4 tablespoons (½ stick) unsalted butter of choice

1 teaspoon raw honey or sugar of choice

1 cup milk of choice

1 (¼-ounce) packet active dry yeast or 2¼ teaspoons active dry yeast

2 cups all-purpose flour, plus more for rolling out the dough

1¾ cups whole wheat flour

1½ teaspoons kosher salt

1 teaspoon baking powder

Nonstick cooking spray

Filling

1½ cups cashews

1 cup boiling water

⅓ cup nutritional yeast

3 tablespoons olive oil

1 teaspoon kosher salt

1 small shallot, finely chopped

2 garlic cloves, minced

1 (14-ounce) can artichoke hearts, drained and roughly chopped

4 cups baby spinach

½ teaspoon dried oregano

¼ teaspoon freshly ground black pepper

¼ teaspoon red pepper flakes

1. **Make the rolls:** In a small saucepan, heat the butter and honey over low heat. Keep over the heat, swirling occasionally, until the butter has melted. Remove from the heat and add the milk. Cool for about 10 minutes until the mixture is warm to the touch, about the temperature of bath water. (If the milk is too hot, it will kill the yeast.)

2. Add the active dry yeast and stir once to combine. Let the mixture sit for about 5 minutes until the yeast is bubbly and fragrant.

3. Meanwhile, in a large bowl. whisk together both flours, the salt, and baking powder.

4. Pour the yeast mixture into the bowl. Use clean hands to swirl the dough together into a cohesive, slightly sticky ball. Knead the dough in the bowl for about 5 minutes until the dough is smooth and taut. Cover with a damp kitchen towel and set somewhere warm to rise until doubled in size, about 1½ hours.

5. **Meanwhile, make the filling:** In a blender, combine the cashews, boiling water, nutritional yeast, 1 tablespoon of the oil, and ½ teaspoon of the salt. Let soak in the blender jar for 30 minutes.

-recipe continues-

6. Meanwhile, in a large skillet, heat the remaining 2 tablespoons oil over medium-high heat. Add the shallot and cook, stirring occasionally, until translucent, about 5 minutes. Add the garlic and cook for about 1 minute more until fragrant. Reduce the heat to medium-low and add the artichokes, spinach, oregano, black pepper, pepper flakes, and remaining ½ teaspoon salt. Cook, stirring occasionally, until the spinach is wilted, about 5 minutes more. Remove from the heat and set aside.

7. After the cashew mixture has soaked, blend on high until a smooth sauce forms, about 1 minute, scraping down the sides as needed. Pour the sauce into the skillet with the spinach and artichoke mixture and return to medium-low heat. Cook for about 5 minutes, stirring occasionally, until the mixture is thick and bubbling. Remove from the heat and set aside to cool completely.

8. When the dough has doubled, punch it down. Cover the bowl with the kitchen towel and set in the refrigerator for 15 minutes.

9. Flour a work surface. Mist a 9 × 13-inch baking pan with nonstick cooking spray. Turn the dough out onto the floured surface. Use a rolling pin to make an 18 × 12-inch rectangle, with the dough about ¼ inch thick. Spread the cooled spinach and artichoke mixture evenly over the dough, leaving a 1-inch border on the 18-inch sides.

10. Start with the 18-inch side facing you and begin to tightly roll the dough over the filling. Continue to roll tightly, starting in the center and working out to the ends. Once the roll is complete, gently pinch along the seam to seal the dough. Slice the dough crosswise into 9 equal rolls and transfer them to the prepared baking pan, leaving plenty of room in between the rows. Cover the pan with a damp kitchen towel and set somewhere warm to rise for about 1 hour, until the rolls have filled the pan.

11. While the rolls are rising, set a rack in the center of the oven and preheat to 400°F.

12. When the rolls are ready, uncover and bake until the rolls are golden brown and firm, 25 to 30 minutes. Let cool in the pan for about 30 minutes before serving warm.

Note • Leftovers can be refrigerated for up to 1 week.

PLANT
This recipe can be made fully vegan.

PLANET
Frozen spinach, thawed and drained, can substitute for fresh spinach. Just adjust the cooking time to 2 minutes to warm the spinach instead of wilting it.

NUTRITION, per serving

| Calories: 440 | Carbs: 52 g | Fiber: 6 g |
| Fat: 22 g | Protein: 14 g | Sugar: 2 g |

Frozen-Fruit Scones

Scones are the mix-and-match heroes of breakfast breads. Almost any bite-size fruit is the right answer. Using frozen fruit means you can enjoy out-of-season flavors without the guilt. And bonus points: Frozen fruit also keeps the dough extra cold for a perfect scone!

1½ cups all-purpose flour

1 cup whole wheat flour

1 teaspoon ground cinnamon

1 teaspoon baking soda

½ teaspoon kosher salt

1 stick (4 ounces) unsalted butter of choice, frozen

Grated zest and juice of 1 lemon

½ cup maple syrup

¼ cup plus 2 tablespoons milk of choice, very cold

1 teaspoon vanilla extract

1 cup frozen fruit, such as blueberries, raspberries, strawberries, or cherries, in any combination

2 teaspoons demerara sugar

1. Set a rack in the center of the oven and preheat to 400°F. Line a sheet pan with a silicone baking mat or parchment paper.

2. In a medium bowl, whisk together both flours, the cinnamon, baking soda, and salt. Use the large holes of a box grater to grate the stick of butter into the flour mixture. Squeeze with clean hands to distribute the butter and create a chunky, sandy flour. Add the lemon zest, lemon juice, maple syrup, ¼ cup of the milk, and the vanilla. Fold the wet ingredients into the flour mixture until just incorporated. Add the fruit and gently fold 2 or 3 times to incorporate.

3. Turn the dough out onto the lined pan and form a 6 × 6-inch square. Cut into 4 squares, then cut each square in half diagonally to create 8 triangles. Separate the triangles and brush with the remaining 2 tablespoons milk and sprinkle with the demerara sugar.

4. Bake until the scones are deep brown, 20 to 25 minutes. (The wheat flour and maple syrup will create a darker color than a traditional scone.) Cool on the pan for 5 minutes before serving.

Note • Leftovers can be refrigerated for up to 1 week.

PLANT
This recipe can be made fully vegan.

PLANET
Frozen fruit is actually better for keeping the dough as cold as possible. Freeze your own fruit in the summer months for a very sustainable scone.

NUTRITION, per serving

Calories: 309	Carbs: 46 g	Fiber: 3 g
Fat: 12 g	Protein: 5 g	Sugar: 15 g

Garden Focaccia

Makes 1 loaf; serves 12

The internet's favorite focaccia is popular for a reason: It's so fun to make! With endless possibilities for decoration, there's no limit to your landscape architecture. Herb sprigs make great stalks and sliced vegetables can be flowers, butterflies, or the sun. Clean out your crisper drawer and go wild!

1 (¼-ounce) packet active dry yeast or 2¼ teaspoons active dry yeast

1 tablespoon sugar of choice or raw honey

2 cups whole wheat flour

1¾ cups all-purpose flour

2 teaspoons kosher salt

5 tablespoons olive oil

Herbs and vegetables, for topping

Flaky sea salt

Edible flowers, for decorating

1. In a large bowl, whisk together the yeast, honey, and 1½ cups warm tap water. Let the yeast bloom for about 5 minutes, until foamy and aromatic.

2. Add the whole wheat flour, all-purpose flour, salt, and 2 tablespoons of the oil. Use a clean hand to swirl the mixture to create a smooth, cohesive dough. Knead the dough in the bowl for about 5 minutes, until it's elastic and the bowl is clean. Cover with a kitchen towel and let it rise in a warm spot until doubled in size, about 2 hours.

3. Set a rack in the center of the oven and preheat to 425°F.

4. Drizzle the remaining 3 tablespoons oil onto a sheet pan. Punch the dough down and turn it out onto the pan. Flip the dough so the oiled side is up and use clean hands to press the dough out toward the edges of the pan. When the dough is spread about halfway, flip it over again so the oily side is facing up. If the dough is pulling back, let it rest for 5 minutes and then resume coaxing it. Once the dough is spread to the edges of the pan, cover the pan with a damp kitchen towel and let the dough rise for about 30 minutes, until puffy.

5. Remove the towel and press your fingers into the dough to create dimples all over the surface. Decorate the dough with herbs, such as sprigs of parsley, dill, and thyme, and vegetables, such as sliced bell peppers, radishes, and cherry tomatoes, creating a garden scene. Sprinkle the dough with flaky sea salt.

6. Bake until golden brown, about 20 minutes. Let the focaccia cool for 10 minutes on the pan before decorating with edible flowers and serving.

Note • Leftovers can be refrigerated for up to 1 week.

PLANT
This recipe is vegan.

PLANET
Adjust the produce to meet the seasons or clean out your fridge.

NUTRITION, per slice

Calories: 188	Carbs: 29 g	Fiber: 3 g
Fat: 6 g	Protein: 5 g	Sugar: 1 g

Sourdough Starter for Beginners

Makes 1 cup

Sourdough was everyone's favorite quar project (too soon?). But if you never jumped on the bandwagon, or you want to keep improving your bread game, this is an easy, manageable starter recipe to get you going. Even if a crackling loaf isn't in your immediate future, there are tons of reasons to have some starter lying around, as you'll see below.

⅓ cup (50 g) bread flour, plus more for feeding

⅓ cup (50 g) whole wheat flour, plus more for feeding

⅓ cup (100 g) warm water, plus more for feeding

1. On Day 1, add the bread flour, whole wheat flour, and warm water to a clear airtight container that can hold at least 2 cups (1 pint). Mix until the flour is fully hydrated, scraping down the sides as needed. Wrap a rubber band or place a piece of tape on the outside of the container to mark the level of the starter. Cover and place in a warm spot for 24 hours.

2. On Day 2, open the container and look for signs of fermentation in the form of bubbles on top, growth past the rubber band, and a yeasty smell. If you see some of these signs, proceed to the next step. If not, cover the starter again and let it sit for another 12 to 24 hours, or until these signs appear.

3. Now it's time to discard and feed. Discard all but about 2 tablespoons of the starter (see Notes on how to minimize waste!). Add another ⅓ cup (100 g) warm water and stir to dissolve the remaining starter. Add ⅓ cup (50 g) bread flour and ⅓ cup (50 g) whole wheat flour and stir until the flour is fully hydrated, scraping down the sides as needed. Adjust the rubber band or tape to mark the new level. Cover and place in a warm spot for another 24 hours.

4. On Days 3 to 15, repeat the discarding and feeding process every day. Eventually, a few hours after feeding, the starter will begin to grow, almost doubling in size, then deflate again. Once your starter is rising and falling regularly, it is in a good place. If you see any fuzzy moldy spots on the surface of your starter that are black, red, or blue, scrape them off the top. If the mold is deeper than surface level, unfortunately you'll need to start over. If the starter develops a dark, clear liquid on top, just pour it off. It's called hooch and it's harmless.

5. Once your starter is up and running, you can keep it at room temperature and feed it daily. Or you can store it in the refrigerator: Do a discard and feed as usual, then refrigerate the starter until you need it. (A refrigerated starter can be fed weekly.) A day before you want to begin making bread, pull the starter out of the refrigerator and let it come to room temperature, about 2 hours. Then discard, feed, and let it ferment for 24 hours.

6. To test the readiness of the starter, do a float test: Fill a cup with cool water. Use a clean spoon to take a scoop of the starter (be careful not to deflate the air bubbles) and carefully plop it in the water. If it floats, it is ready for baking! If not, try again a few hours later or continue the feeding process for a few more days.

7. After passing the float test, the starter is ready to use for baking! A young starter, one that passes the float test a few hours after feeding, will be a little sweeter. A mature starter, usually about 6 to 12 hours after feeding, will have a more sour, fermented taste. Both are excellent.

Notes • It may be tempting not to discard most of your starter every time you feed it because you don't want to waste it, but refreshing the flour and water is the most important part of making a starter. To cut back on waste, keep a designated discard container in the refrigerator and fill it up. The discard can be mixed into pancakes, pizza dough, biscuits, pie dough, banana bread, and cookies. It will last up to 3 months in the refrigerator or 1 year in the freezer.

Active starters can last for years if properly fed.

PLANT
This recipe is vegan.

PLANET
Everything in this recipe can be sustainably purchased year-round and might even be sitting in your pantry already.

Sourdough Bread for Beginners

Baking bread can be tough, but a good starter is half the battle. From there it's all about treating your dough right to create strong gluten. (Developing the gluten gives your bread structure, rise, and those beautiful bubbles in the crumb.) A lot of bread bakers learn by doing, and failing, over time, so don't get discouraged if your first loaf isn't perfect. Worst case, you have some incredible croutons or bread crumbs in your future.

⅔ cup (400 g) plus 1 tablespoon (15 g) warm water

½ cup (113 g) Sourdough Starter for Beginners (page 240)

3 cups (450 g) bread flour, plus more for the work surface

⅔ cup (100 g) whole wheat flour

1 tablespoon (8.4 g) kosher salt

1. In a medium bowl, combine ⅔ cup of the warm water and the starter and stir with a rubber spatula to dissolve the starter. Add the bread flour and whole wheat flour. Use a spatula or clean hands to mix until the flour is fully hydrated. Cover with a clean kitchen towel and rest in a warm place for about 1 hour. You should see signs of fermentation, an increase in volume, and bubbles along the top of the dough. Wait about 30 minutes more if fermentation isn't visible.

2. After resting the dough, add the salt and remaining 1 tablespoon of water. Set a bowl of water nearby. Use clean hands to incorporate the salt, squeezing the dough through your fingers to make sure it is evenly distributed. Once the salt is incorporated, dip your hands in the water to prevent sticking. Use your wet hands to stretch the dough from the edge of the bowl upward, then fold toward the center. Repeat a total of 8 times, rotating the bowl slightly after each fold.

3. After the folds, carefully lift the dough up, flip it over, place it back in the bowl, and tuck the edges under. Scrape down the edges of the bowl as needed, then cover with the same kitchen towel and rest in a warm place for 1 hour more, until fermentation is visible.

4. Repeat the stretching and folding process 2 more times, covering and resting for about 1 hour after each folding session before beginning again.

5. An hour after the final stretch and fold, it's time to shape. Dip clean hands in the water again. Think of the dough as the face of a clock. Slide your hands into the bowl at 3 o'clock and 9 o'clock. Partially lift the dough from the bowl and let it fold under itself as you place it down. Rotate the bowl and repeat the lifting and fold under 5 or 6 times, until the dough has begun to come together in a ball. Carefully lift the dough onto a clean surface. Lightly sprinkle the dough with more bread flour. Using a bench scraper or lightly floured hands, carefully

rotate and drag the dough toward you along the surface, building tension until you have a round, taut ball of dough. Do not make the ball too tight, as it may tear. Lightly flour the dough with more bread flour, cover with the towel, and rest for about 30 minutes, until relaxed and slightly spread.

6. Dust a proofing basket with bread flour. (Alternatively, line a medium bowl with a cotton towel and dust it with flour.) Using the bench scraper or lightly floured hands, carefully flip the dough upside down. Think of the clock again. Fold in 12 o'clock toward the center, then 6 o'clock, 3 o'clock, and 9 o'clock, then each of the remaining 4 diagonal corners. Carefully transfer the dough, seam-side up, to the prepared proofing basket (or bowl). Pinch the seams to ensure they are sealed. Cover the basket (or bowl) with the towel. Transfer the dough to the refrigerator to finish proofing overnight, 12 to 18 hours.

7. Set a rack in the center of the oven and preheat to 500°F. Cut out a piece of parchment paper that's about 1 inch wider than the lid of your Dutch oven and set aside. Place the Dutch oven and lid in the oven. Preheat for at least 30 minutes before baking.

8. Place the cut-out piece of parchment over the proofing basket or bowl and gently flip the basket over so the dough drops onto the parchment. Remove the Dutch oven from the oven and open the lid. Use the parchment paper to carefully lower the dough into the Dutch oven. Use a sharp paring knife or bread lame (razor) to score the top of the dough a few times, which will allow steam to escape. Cover the Dutch oven and carefully return to the oven.

9. Bake until the bread has risen, about 25 minutes. Uncover the Dutch oven and reduce the oven temperature to 450°F. Continue baking until the crust is golden brown, another 15 to 20 minutes.

10. Remove the bread from the oven and use the parchment paper to carefully transfer the dough to a wire rack. Check to make sure it is done baking by tapping on the bottom—it should sound hollow. Cool completely, at least 2 hours, before slicing with a serrated knife. Store the loaf cut-side down on a cutting board or in a bread bag for up to 3 days. (You can freeze the whole loaf, or freeze slices, for up to 3 months.)

Note • Make several loaves and freeze them for later.

PLANT
This recipe is vegan.

PLANET
Everything in this recipe can be sustainably purchased year-round and might even be sitting in your pantry already.

NUTRITION, per slice

| Calories: 149 | Carbs: 31 g | Fiber: 3 g |
| Fat: 1 g | Protein: 5 g | Sugar: 0 g |

Dairy & Vegan Butter

Makes 1 cup

Butter! Nothing elevates a slice of bread (or steamed vegetables or cooked pasta or—you get it) like butter. Homemade dairy butter is impossibly simple with a few spins of the food processor. And a great vegan spread can go from pantry items to refrigerator with one quick blast in the blender. It's a win no matter how you slice it.

Dairy butter

2 cups heavy cream

1 tablespoon yogurt

Kosher salt (optional)

1. In a food processor, combine the cream and yogurt and process for about 5 minutes, until the mixture gets thick and then the butter solids separate. Pour the buttermilk liquid into a clean jar and set aside.

2. Scoop the butter solids into a clean tea towel and squeeze over the sink to release any remaining liquid. Wash the butter under cold water and squeeze again. Repeat until the liquid runs clear. (Any milk left in the butter will spoil it faster.)

3. Knead a pinch of salt into the butter if you want it salted. Transfer to a storage container, or wrap it tightly, and refrigerate for up to 2 weeks. Refrigerate the buttermilk in the jar for up to 1 week.

Vegan butter

¼ cup milk of choice

½ teaspoon apple cider vinegar

¾ cup refined coconut oil

2 tablespoons vegetable oil

½ teaspoon nutritional yeast

¼ teaspoon kosher salt

Pinch of ground turmeric

In a blender or food processor, combine the milk and vinegar and let sit for about 2 minutes to curdle. Add the coconut oil, vegetable oil, nutritional yeast, salt, and a small pinch of turmeric for color. Blend on high to form a smooth mixture, about 1 minute. Pour into a chilled storage container and refrigerate until firm, about 2 hours. Store in the refrigerator for up to 2 weeks.

PLANT
This recipe can be made vegetarian or vegan.

PLANET
Everything in this recipe can be sustainably purchased year-round, just shop wisely.

NUTRITION, per 1 tablespoon

Calories: 102
Fat: 11 g

Carbs: 1 g
Protein: 1 g

Fiber: 0 g
Sugar: 1 g

Sweet Potato Seed Loaf

Makes 1 loaf; serves 8

Free of everything—grains, dairy, eggs, refined sugar—but still moist and sweet like a loaf should be! Walnuts, pumpkin seeds, oats, and coconut bring the texture, while all the best spices enhance the creamy sweet potato. Raisins and maple syrup round out the sweetness, making it equally great for breakfast or dessert!

1 cup raw walnuts

1 cup raw pumpkin seeds

2 cups old-fashioned rolled oats

1 cup unsweetened coconut flakes

1 cup raisins

1 cup milk of choice

½ cup maple syrup

¼ cup olive oil

¼ cup chia seeds

1 (15-ounce) can sweet potato puree or 1¾ cups mashed and cooled sweet potato

1 cup flaxseed meal

2 teaspoons kosher salt

1 teaspoon baking powder

1 teaspoon baking soda

2 teaspoons ground cinnamon

1 teaspoon ground ginger

¼ teaspoon ground nutmeg

¼ teaspoon ground cloves

1 tablespoon refined coconut oil

1. In a food processor or blender, combine the walnuts and pumpkin seeds and pulse 4 or 5 times to break them down into coarse pieces. Transfer to a large bowl.

2. Add the oats and coconut flakes to the food processor or blender and process for about 1 minute to make a coarse flour. Add the raisins, milk, maple syrup, and olive oil and continue to process until a thick paste forms, about 1 minute, scraping down the sides as needed.

3. Transfer the mixture to the same large bowl as the nuts. Add the chia seeds, sweet potato, flaxseed meal, salt, baking powder, baking soda, cinnamon, ginger, nutmeg, and cloves. Use a spatula to fold into a thick batter.

4. Rub a 9 × 5-inch loaf pan with the coconut oil. Transfer the batter to the pan, smoothing the top. Cover loosely with a kitchen towel and let it sit at room temperature for 2 hours.

5. Set a rack in the center of the oven and preheat to 400°F.

6. Remove the towel and set the loaf pan on a baking sheet. Bake until the loaf has risen slightly and turned deep brown, about 1 hour.

7. Remove from the oven and cool completely in the pan, about 1 hour, before serving. (Alternatively, cool completely, wrap tightly, and store in the refrigerator to enjoy all week.)

PLANT
This recipe is vegan.

PLANET
Sweet potato is in season during the fall and winter months, but canned sweet potato works great in other months.

NUTRITION, per serving

| Calories: 675 | Carbs: 62 g | Fiber: 13 g |
| Fat: 33 g | Protein: 10 g | Sugar: 33 g |

Notes

Shopping Seasonally

13 **Seasonal produce tastes better:** "The Benefits of Eating Seasonal Produce." *Brighter Bites*, 12 Aug. 2015, brighterbites.org/news /benefits-eating-seasonal-produce

14 **An incredible resource:** *Seasonal Food Guide*, GRACE Communications Foundation, 2020, seasonalfoodguide.org

14 **According to the USDA:** "Seasonal Produce Guide." *SNAP Education Connection*, GRACE Communications Foundation, 2020, snaped.fns .usda.gov/seasonal-produce-guide

Shopping Sustainably

17 **In almost (almost!) all cases, the USDA:** "Electronic Code of Federal Regulations." *Electronic Code of Federal Regulations (ECFR)*, 23 Nov. 2020, ecfr.federalregister.gov

17 **But any food prominently featuring the word:** "Labeling Organic Products." *Agriculture Marketing Service*, Oct. 2012, ams.usda .gov/sites/default/files/media/Labeling%20 Organic%20Products%20Fact%20Sheet.pdf

17 **The other major label that sustainable and plant-based:** "Non-GMO Project Verification Guide." *Non-GMO Project*, Jan. 2020, nongmoproject.org/wp-content/uploads /Verification-Guide.pdf

18 **Without a labeled certification:** A Greener World. "Certified Animal Welfare Approved by AGW Food Label." *A Greener World*, agreenerworld.org/certifications/animal -welfare-approved

18 **This label guarantees:** "Electronic Code of Federal Regulations." *Electronic Code of Federal Regulations (ECFR)*, 23 Nov. 2020, ecfr.federalregister.gov

18 **This collective of farmers peer-reviews:** "Who We Are." *Certified Naturally Grown (CNG)*, 2015, www.cngfarming.org/who_we_are

18 **based on the same exacting guidelines:** "Produce & Flowers Certification." *Certified Naturally Grown (CNG)*, 2015, cngfarming.org /produce

18 **without all the bureaucratic paperwork:** "Frequently Asked Questions." *Certified Naturally Grown (CNG)*, 2015, cngfarming .org/faqs

19 **CNG offers small farmers credit for the work:** "FAQs." *Certified Naturally Grown (CNG)*, 2015, www.cngfarming.org/faqs

19 **two items that are difficult to certify:** "Organic Labeling." *Organic Labeling | Agricultural Marketing Service*, www.ams.usda .gov/rules-regulations/organic/labeling

19 **The Certified Naturally Grown label follows:** "Livestock Standards." *Certified Naturally Grown (CNG)*, 2015, cngfarming.org/livestock _standards

19 **chickens who are no longer laying eggs:** "Poultry and Eggs: Industries That Abuse Chickens." *PETA*, 17 Apr. 2020, peta.org/issues /animals-used-for-food/animals-used-food -factsheets/poultry-eggs-industries-abuse -chickens

19 **Animal Welfare Approved by A Greener World:** Carrier, Tobias. "Laying Hen Standards." *A Greener World*, agreenerworld.org /certifications/animal-welfare-approved /standards/laying-hen-standards

19   **They guarantee: Non-GMO animal feed:** "Electronic Code of Federal Regulations." *Electronic Code of Federal Regulations (ECFR)*, ecfr.federalregister.gov

20   **Certified Grassfed by A Greener World:** "Certified Grassfed by A Greener World standards for beef, sheep, dairy sheep, goats, dairy goats and bison." *A Greener World*, agreenerworld.org/wp-content/uploads/2018/05 /Certified-Grassfed-by-AGW-standards-2018.pdf

20   **Pennsylvania Certified Organic Grass-Fed:** "Certification Manual." Pennsylvania Certified Organic, *Earth Claims LLC*, 1 Jul. 2019, paorganic .org/wp-content/uploads/2020/01/OPT-PCO -OPT-Grass-Fed-Certification-Manual1.pdf

20   **Northeast Organic Farming Association Certified:** *Additional Services & Certifications - NOFA-NY - Northeast Organic Farming Association of New York*. 23 Apr. 2020, nofany.org/certification/additional-services -certifications

20   **USDA Organic/Pros:** "Electronic Code of Federal Regulations." *Electronic Code of Federal Regulations (ECFR)*, 23 Nov. 2020, ecfr.federalregister.gov

22   **In terms of milk alternatives:** Held, Lisa. "Which Plant-Based Milk Is Best for the Environment?" *Edible Brooklyn*, 31 Jan. 2020, ediblebrooklyn .com/2020/plant-milks-sustainability

22   **Food Justice Certification by the Agricultural Justice Project:** "Food Justice Certification for Farmers." *Agricultural Justice Project*, agriculturaljusticeproject.org/media /uploads/2017/03/15/2015.1.15.AJP_Introduction _to_Farmer_Practices_for_printing.pdf

Shopping Package-Free

25   **1 and 5 trillion plastic bags:** Ekvall, Tomas, et al. "Single-use plastic bags and their alternatives: Recommendations from Life Cycle Assessments." *Life Cycle Initiative*, United Nations Environment Programme, 2020, lifecycleinitiative.org /wp-content/uploads/2020/04/Single -use-plastic-bags-and-alternatives -Recommendations-from-LCA-final.pdf

25   **380 billion plastic bags:** Anderson, Marcia. "Confronting Plastic Pollution One Bag at a Time." *EPA*, Environmental Protection Agency, 1 Nov. 2016, blog.epa.gov/2016/11/01/confronting -plastic-pollution-one-bag-at-a-time

25   **4.14 million tons of plastic bags:** "Advancing Sustainable Materials Management: 2016 and 2017 Tables and Figures." *EPA*, Environmental Protection Agency, Nov. 2019, epa.gov/sites /production/files/2019-11/documents/2016 _and_2017_facts_and_figures_data_tables _0.pdf

26   **a process called photodegradation:** "Turning the Tide on Trash: A Learning Guide on Marine Debris." *Marine Debris Program*, National Oceanic and Atmospheric Administration, Nov. 2019, marinedebris.noaa.gov/sites/default/files /publications-files/2015_TurningTideonTrash _HiRes_Final.pdf

26   **90 pounds of plastic blocking:** Borunda, Alejandra. "This Young Whale Died with 88 Pounds of Plastic in Its Stomach." *National Geographic*, 18 Mar. 2019, nationalgeographic .com/environment/2019/03/whale-dies-88 -pounds-plastic-philippines/?mod=article_inline

26   **More than half of all dead sea turtles:** Anderson, Marcia. "Confronting Plastic Pollution One Bag at a Time." *EPA*, Environmental Protection Agency, 1 Nov. 2016, blog.epa .gov/2016/11/01/confronting-plastic-pollution -one-bag-at-a-time

27   **here are five easy ways to increase your impact:** "Ten Ways to Unpackage Your Life." *EPA*, Environmental Protection Agency, 14 Sept. 2020, epa.gov/trash-free-waters/ten-ways -unpackage-your-life

A Sustainable Budget

29   **we spend an average of 9.7 percent:** "Food Prices and Spending." *Economic Research Service*, USDA, 6 Nov. 2020, ers.usda.gov/data -products/ag-and-food-statistics-charting-the -essentials/food-prices-and-spending

29   **when the average American household was spending:** Chao, Elaine L., and Kathleen P. Utgoff. "100 Years of U.S. Consumer Spending: Data for the Nation, New York City, and Boston." US Bureau of Labor Statistics, 3 Aug. 2006, bls.gov /opub/100-years-of-u-s-consumer-spending.pdf

30   **The average American throws away about 238 pounds:** "How to Talk About Food Waste." *FFA New Horizons*, National FFA Organization, 17 May 2019, ffa.org/ffa-new-horizons/how-to -talk-about-food-waste

33   *Forbes* **recently did a study:** "Here's How Much Money You Save by Cooking at Home." Priceonomics, *Forbes*, 10 July 2018, forbes.com /sites/priceonomics/2018/07/10/heres-how -much-money-do-you-save-by-cooking-at-home

Grow Your Own

38   **Save all nondairy food scraps:** *Compost Food Scraps.* GrowNYC, grownyc.org/compost

38   **Start saving other biodegradable materials:** *Compost Food Scraps.* GrowNYC, grownyc.org /compost

Make It Stretch

39   **Nearly 40 percent of food goes to waste:** "NRDC: A Holistic Approach to Reducing Food Waste." *Natural Resources Defense Council*, Jan. 2019, nrdc.org/sites/default/files/holistic -approach-reducing-food-waste-fs.pdf

39   **staying below 40°F:** "4 Steps to Food Safety." *FoodSafety.gov*, U.S. Department of Health & Human Services, 21 Nov. 2019, foodsafety.gov /keep-food-safe/4-steps-to-food-safety

39   **The freezer should be kept at 0°F:** "4 Steps to Food Safety." *FoodSafety.gov*, U.S. Department of Health & Human Services, 21 Nov. 2019, foodsafety.gov/keep-food-safe/4-steps-to-food- safety

40   **think about your unit in zones:** Han, Emily. "Where to Store What in the Refrigerator." *Kitchn*, Apartment Therapy, LLC., 2 May 2019, thekitchn.com/where-to-store-what-in-the -ref-130438

Acknowledgments

A massive thank-you to everyone who contributes to Goodful!

Author & Original Recipe Developer

Casey Elsass

Recipe Tester

Karlee Rotoly

Contributing Producers

Katie Aubin

Marissa Buie

Greg Perez

Karlee Rotoly

Alix Traeger

Everyone at Goodful

Emily DePaula

Eric Karp

Jay Fleckenstein

Devon McGowan

Ines Pacheco

Ivy Tai

And the entire Goodful and BuzzFeed team

Photography & Styling

David Malosh

Simon Andrews

Paige Hicks

Spencer Richards

Index

Library of Congress Cataloging-in-Publication Data
is available upon request.

ISBN 978-0-593-13551-8
Ebook ISBN 978-0-593-13552-5

Printed in China

Photographer: David Malosh
Editor: Donna Loffredo
Designer: Jan Derevjanik
Illustrator: Jay Fleckenstein
Production Editor: Patricia Shaw
Production Manager: Heather Williamson
Composition: Merri Ann Morrell and Nick Patton
Copy Editor: Kate Slate
Indexer: Thérèse Shere

10 9 8 7 6 5 4 3 2 1

First Edition